Learning WML & WMLScript

Learning WML & WMLScript

Martin Frost

O'REILLY®

Beijing · Cambridge · Farnham · Köln · Paris · Sebastopol · Taipei · Tokyo

Learning WML and WMLScript
by Martin Frost

Copyright © 2000 O'Reilly & Associates, Inc. All rights reserved.
Printed in the United States of America.

Published by O'Reilly & Associates, Inc., 101 Morris Street, Sebastopol, CA 95472.

Editor: John Posner

Production Editor: Mary Anne Weeks Mayo

Cover Designer: Ellie Volckhausen

Printing History:

      October 2000:   First Edition.

CIP data can be found at *http://www.oreilly.com/catalog/learnwml.*

ISBN: 1-56592-947-0
[M]

Table of Contents

Preface

The Wireless Application Protocol (WAP) is an industry-wide specification for applications that operate over wireless networks, with particular emphasis on applications for mobile devices, especially mobile phones. The standards are published by the WAP Forum, a body formed in June 1997 by Ericsson, Nokia, Motorola, and Unwired Planet, which has since been joined by over a hundred other companies, including IBM, Hewlett-Packard, Visa, and Microsoft. According to the WAP Forum's official statistics, WAP Forum members represent over 90% of cellular-phone manufacturers worldwide.

WAP will be supported by many kinds of devices, from simple cell phones similar to those available today to a new generation of "smart" phones with large touch screens and many applications of their own. That's before we even look at the range of personal digital assistants (PDAs) available, from palmtops to full miniaturized computers complete with keyboards. All will eventually get WAP capabilities, either directly from the manufacturer or as some sort of third-party upgrade. Each device has a different kind of display and different methods for user input. The job of the WAP specification is to sort out this mess and provide a common framework to allow applications to run across all these different platforms.

Since WAP works in a mobile environment, it also has to contend with the particular problems of wireless networks: low bandwidth (9600 bps or less is commonplace), high latency (round-trip times of the order of seconds are not uncommon), and unreliability (someone may be using her WAP phone when the train goes into a tunnel or when she walks past a tall building). Everyone with a mobile phone knows about the reliability problems.

These problems are why WAP is necessary. Some people may ask why they can't just have normal web pages delivered over normal TCP/IP connections, the only difference from their PCs at home being the wireless link. The trouble with the normal web technologies is that they are aimed at high bandwidth and big screens. WAP keeps the Internet model but optimizes each component for a mobile environment. It keeps track of the state of a session in case the connection is lost, provides compressed formats for the transferred data, and handles displaying of applications regardless of the input and output available.

The WAP Stack

The term that refers to all the different parts of the WAP specifications is the *WAP stack*. This is because the components can conceptually be thought of as layers in a stack. The user interacts with the top of the stack, and the communications hardware sits below the lowest level. This concept is illustrated in Figure P-1, together with the names of the various specifications involved.

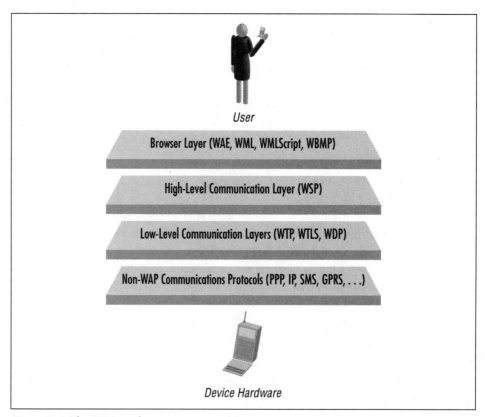

Figure P-1. The WAP stack

Going from bottom to top, the lowest layer in the figure contains various protocols (the so-called *bearer* protocols), which aren't actually part of WAP but which provide the link between WAP and the actual communications hardware:

- *IP* (Internet Protocol) and *PPP* (Point to Point Protocol) are the two lowest-level protocols in normal dialup Internet access. (Many first-generation WAP devices work by making a normal dialup call and sending the WAP data across a modem link. IP and PPP are used in such a case.)

- *SMS* (Short Message Service) is a feature provided by most digital mobile phone systems that allows short messages to be sent and received across the wireless link. (Users see this as the ability to send short text messages—a bit like email.) It can also transmit binary data and be used for WAP.

- *GPRS* (General Packet Radio System) is a next-generation mobile phone system that will bring higher bandwidth and permanent network connections to cell phones and other wireless devices. Instead of having to dial into the server, a cell phone will effectively have a permanent Internet connection. GPRS is based on IP.

The next layer up includes various low-level WAP communications protocols: *WTP* (Wireless Transaction Protocol), *WTLS* (Wireless Transaction Layer Security), and *WDP* (Wireless Datagram Protocol). WTP and WDP provide low-level glue between the upper levels and the really low-level communications. WTLS provides security services (encryption and authentication). These protocols aren't relevant to normal application programmers: unless you're designing a browser, you don't need to know about them.

The second highest level in the stack is the high-level communications protocol, called *WSP* (Wireless Session Protocol). This provides a complete replacement for *HTTP* (HyperText Transfer Protocol), which is the protocol used between web servers and web browsers. Although you don't need to know how this layer works, there are one or two features that may be directly useful: these are described in Appendix B, *WAP Gateways and WSP*.

The highest stack level is the *WAE* (Wireless Application Environment), which is the part that the user actually sees and with which she interacts. The WAE aims to provide a World Wide Web–like model for writing applications, allowing existing web developers to ease the transition to producing content and applications for mobile devices.

To achieve this, the WAE incorporates several key features of the Web that you'll be familiar with, including *URLs* (like *http://www.wap.net*) and *MIME content types* (such as `text/html` and `image/gif`. Additionally, it provides similar replacements for other features: HTML is replaced with *WML* (Wireless Markup Language), and JavaScript is replaced with *WMLScript* (Wireless Markup Language Script). Almost all WAP applications can be written without using anything outside of these two languages and *WBMP* (Wireless Bitmap: the WAP image format), so they form the vast majority of what you as a developer need to know (and the vast majority of this book!).

From Server to Client

The complete chain of processing that occurs to WAP content on its journey to the user is illustrated in Figure P-2. (This figure omits the details of the communications, since they're not very important, and they change depending on the precise low-level bearer protocol in use.)

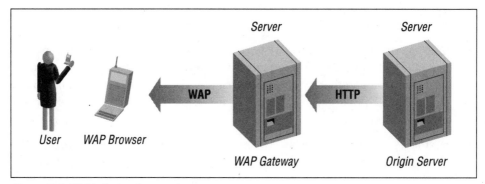

Figure P-2. WAP chain of processing

The WAP browser in the figure can run on any supported device, from a cell phone to a PDA. Generally, cell phones need to be designed to support WAP, but most modern PDAs can be upgraded to support WAP simply by purchasing the browser software and installing it. PDAs need to be used with a cell phone to provide the connectivity.

The origin server (on the far right of the figure) stores or generates the content itself. In nearly all cases, the protocol used to communicate with the origin server is standard HTTP, so this can be a standard web server. It's usually necessary to make a couple of minor modifications* to the server's configuration, so it can serve WAP content. All the most popular web-server software can perform this task. An interesting solution is to use a technology such as *XSLT* (XML Stylesheet Language Transformations), which allows both HTML and WML to be automatically generated from the same raw data.

Not included in the picture but quite likely to be present is some sort of backend database server. The origin server uses standard web technologies (such as CGI scripts or Java servlets, for instance) to generate any required dynamic content. These scripts probably need to communicate with a database to get the raw data to output. (This is going beyond the scope of this book, however. All standard

---

* Specifically, modifications include adding support for the WAP content types. The types that need to be added are described in Appendix D, *Serving WAP Content from a Standard Web Server*.

techniques for generating web content on a server will also work for WAP, so you should read a book on one of those.)

The WAP Gateway

The WAP gateway box in Figure P-2 is the more interesting. The job of the WAP gateway is to convert between the browser's WAP communication protocols (WSP, WTP, and so on) and the standard HTTP and TCP/IP protocols required by the origin server. It's also responsible for converting the content output by the origin server (formatted as text) into the compressed binary formats of WML and WML-Script as required by the browser.

The gateway consists of some software to do this conversion, usually running on some sort of standard hardware. (Most proper gateways run on heavy-duty Unix servers, but there is low-end gateway software available that even runs on a Windows-based PC.) The gateway's owner must also handle the connection to the bearer network. For a dialup-based bearer, this process is achieved through a standard access server (the same pieces of hardware people use to dial in to the Internet), but for such bearers as SMS and GPRS, the connection will probably involve a leased line to a carrier.

Because of all these infrastructure requirements, most people offering WAP content will not run their own gateways. (Many people will run their own origin servers, since this is not much different from running a normal web server, but far fewer people will run full WAP gateways.) All cell phone carriers that want to support WAP (which is most of them) will probably run their own gateways, and a number of other portal sites already exist, which also run gateways. Since most of these allow users to connect to any content on the Internet, a user just needs an account on one of these to access all the third-party content available.

This Book

This book doesn't aim to cover the low-level details of either the communication protocols (from your perspective, they behave just like HTTP) or the compressed file formats (it doesn't matter to you how your application gets to the device; all that matters is that it does). I also don't go into the details of how security and encryption are handled (these are just other parts of the communication process). Most web developers don't bother to learn how HTTP or TCP/IP work, as they can get by just fine without, and it only distracts them from their real job of writing web pages. If you want to know these details, you can download the latest versions of the specifications from the WAP Forum's web site (*http://www. wapforum.org*).

Conventions Used in This Book

This book uses the following font conventions:

Italic

> Indicates operating-system pathnames; filenames; program names; Internet addresses, such as domain names and URLs; and new terms where they are defined.

Boldface

> Indicates names of GUI items: window names, buttons, menu choices, etc.

`Constant width`

> Indicates code, command lines, and options that should be typed verbatim; names and keywords in WML and WMLScript programs, including function names and variable names; and XML element tags.

`*Italic constant width*`

> Indicates items in code where the user or programmer must supply a name or value.

> The owl icon designates a note, which is an important aside to the nearby text.

> The turkey icon designates a warning relating to the nearby text.

Comments and Questions

The information in this book has been tested and verified, but you may find that features have changed (or you may even find mistakes!). You can send any errors you find, as well as suggestions for future editions, to:

> O'Reilly & Associates, Inc.
> 101 Morris Street
> Sebastopol, CA 95472
> (800) 998-9938 (in the United States or Canada)
> (707) 829-0515 (international/local)
> (707) 829-0104 (fax)

You can also send messages electronically. To be put on the mailing list or request a catalog, send email to:

> *info@oreilly.com*

To ask technical questions or comment on the book, send email to:

> *bookquestions@oreilly.com*

There is a web site for the book, where examples, errata, and any plans for future editions are listed. The site also includes a link to a forum where you can discuss the book with the author and other readers. You can access this site at:

> *http://www.oreilly.com/catalog/learnwml*

For more information about this book and others, see the O'Reilly web site:

> *http://www.oreilly.com*

Acknowledgments

As ever, this book involves the work of many people besides myself.

I am deeply grateful to my editor, John Posner, for his continual constructive criticism and innumerable helpful comments. Without them, this book would be vastly inferior. I really can't emphasize enough how great a help he was. Thanks to Christien Shangraw and Katie Gardner for finding and supplying me with the StarOffice template and for responding patiently to my queries. Thanks are also due to O'Reilly in general, for allowing me the opportunity to write this book.

Thanks and apologies must go to my friends, who put up with me cancelling plans weekend after weekend so that I could get some writing done. Thanks especially to all the people who offered to read through the book before I sent it off: sorry that I never got any of it finished early enough to take you up on your offers!

A small and select group of people have been particularly understanding in the face of almost complete abandonment to The Book. You know who you are.

Thanks to my employer, for allowing me to write the book in the first place and for allowing me time off at short notice when deadlines were approaching.

Finally, a special thanks must go to Leon, because of the quantity of beer he promised me if I'd give him a mention.

1

Introduction to WML

The heart of WAP from the point of view of you, the content developer, is a new markup language called the Wireless Markup Language (WML). If you have worked with the HyperText Markup Language (HTML), much of WML will look familiar but be warned that there are several differences that can easily catch you out. Some of these differences come from WML's simplicity compared to HTML: many features that are found in HTML are simply not present in WML.

To use a common example, HTML gives you great control over the appearance of text within a document: you can change its size, specify the typeface to be used, add styling such as boldface or underlining, and have a fine degree of control over its color.

The only controls WML gives you over the text are a few simple styles (emphasis, strong emphasis, boldface, italics, and underlining) and the ability to specify text that is larger or smaller than normal. A further surprise is that most WAP browsers to date don't even support most of these.

Losing this control over appearance that HTML provides forces you to think in a different way about the pages you write, concentrating on content rather than appearance (substance over style, if you like). If you've ever designed a web page to be usable under a really old browser (or a text-only browser) as well as the latest version of a major browser, you'll already have a good idea of the sort of things you need to bear in mind. Not all browsers even know about recent HTML such features as tables, frames, or stylesheets, and if you want to support people with those browsers, you have three choices: avoid the new feature altogether, write your pages to work even if the feature isn't present, or provide multiple versions of your pages and allow the user to select his favorite combination of features. In the same way, not all WAP browsers support images, tables, or text style changes,* and if you rely on them, you reduce the potential audience for your pages dramatically.

It's not all bad, though. While WML does drop many of the features of HTML, it adds some powerful new ones, and because it was designed from the start for interactive applications many of the headaches of the web world simply disappear. It also has the advantage of having been designed in one go, rather than having features haphazardly added by different people without any proper overall coordination, which is the case with many of the new features of HTML.

A Complete Example

Before we discuss WML any further, Example 1-1 displays the time-honored "Hello World." The code for this example, as well as all the other substantial examples, is available on the book's web page (*http://www.oreilly.com/catalog/learnwml*).

Example 1-1. A Simple WML Example

```
<?xml version="1.0"?>
<!DOCTYPE wml PUBLIC
    "-//WAPFORUM//DTD WML 1.1//EN"
    "http://www.wapforum.org/DTD/wml_1.1.xml">

<wml>
    <card title="First WML Example">
        <p>Hello, World!</p>
    </card>
</wml>
```

Depending on the browser in use, this may look something like Figure 1-1.

Several things need to be explained about this example, but for some of them you'll have to wait until later chapters. The first thing to note is the special header (the first four lines). This looks confusing, but you don't actually need to know what it means: just include it at the top of all your WML pages, and all the programs that deal with them will be happy.†

The second thing to note is that all tag names are in lowercase (tags are inside angle brackets). This is important: unlike HTML, where `<HTML>`, `<html>`, `<Html>`,

---

* There are several reasons why these features may not be available. One is that some displays may simply be unable to cope with the features. Another reason, which is common at the moment but which will hopefully go away in the future, is that less widely used features were often lost in the rush to get a WAP device out into the market as early as possible.

† If you're familiar with the eXtensible Markup Language (XML), you'll recognize these lines as the *XML prolog* for the document. (WML is an *XML application*, which means that WML documents follow a set of rules laid down in the XML specifications.) If you're don't know XML, it doesn't matter: just copy those four lines and live in blissful ignorance. A number of other parts of WML syntax are also derived from XML: I will point these out as we encounter them.

Figure 1-1. Example 1-1 displayed in a WAP browser

and <hTMl> all refer to the same thing, in WML, tag names are *case-sensitive*. All current WML tag names are lowercase, so you must enter them that way in your pages.

If you've seen some HTML, the rest of the WML syntax should look vaguely familiar, although the first tag is <wml>, not <HTML>, and there's that mysterious-looking <card> tag. The <p> tag simply starts a paragraph of text (in this simple case, there is only the one).

Cards

The reason for the <card> tag is that WML structures its content differently from HTML. Instead of a file being a long stream of content, a file of WML represents a *deck of cards.* Only one card is displayed at a time, but you can link from one card to another and store several in a deck in the same file. Each individual card does in fact behave very much like an HTML page, so you can think of a WML deck as being similar to a number of HTML pages all grouped together. It's good WML style to use decks of cards to group together related information or user interactions. Cards in a deck are all downloaded at the same time, so the user has to wait only once, and the others can be accessed almost instantly.

Conversely, it's bad WML style to overuse cards, cramming too many into a single deck (and hence into a single downloaded file). Even if you think 30 cards of information are all relevant at the same time, the user will get bored waiting for all of them to download before she gets to see the first one. It is hard to put a fixed limit on the number of cards you should use, but here's a general rule of thumb: if you find yourself using more than five or six cards in a single deck, you should think hard about how your pages are organized. Although you shouldn't concern yourself too much with the transmission of the content, another thing to bear in mind is that many devices can't cope with large files. (The Nokia 7110 cell phone, the most popular WAP device in Europe, has trouble if the deck is more than about 1400 bytes after being passed through the gateway.)

Empty-Element Tags

Now, just to worry all the HTML users some more, check out Example 1-2.

Example 1-2. An Interesting Tag

```
<?xml version="1.0"?>
<!DOCTYPE wml PUBLIC
    "-//WAPFORUM//DTD WML 1.1//EN"
    "http://www.wapforum.org/DTD/wml_1.1.xml">

<wml>
    <card title="Another WML Example">
        <p><img src="img/pic.wbmp" alt="Image"/></p>
    </card>
</wml>
```

You should recognize most of the structure from Example 1-1, and the `<img>` tag may be familiar from HTML, but look more closely at the end of the tag: note the extra slash. This is required in WML whenever a tag has no matching end-tag. (An end-tag has a slash after the first angle bracket, like `</end>`.) These so-called *empty-element tags* are quite common in both WML and HTML, but HTML doesn't decorate them in any special way, so they look just like start-tags. This makes some unnecessary work for the browser and any other program that has to read the file, so WML makes the structure more consistent.*

Elements

An alternative way of thinking about these extra slashes is to think in terms of *elements*.† An element takes one of two forms: either a start-tag and an end-tag (whose types must match):

```
<tag> . . . </tag>
```

or a single empty-element tag (complete with extra slash):

```
<tag/>
```

Note that there is exactly one slash per element.

An element can contain other elements (either matched pairs or empty-element tags), possibly mixed up with flow text. Looking at Example 1-2 this way, there is a single <wml> element (as a matched pair <wml> </wml>), containing a single <card> element (as a matched pair <card> </card>), containing a single <p> element (also as a matched pair, <p> </p>), which in turn contains a single <img> element (as the empty-element tag <img/>).

It's important to ensure the tags match properly. Mismatching tags such as:

```
<x>...<y>...</x>...</y>
```

is an error and will prevent the page from being displayed. This should have been written as:

```
<x>...<y>...</y>...</x>
```

Attributes

Start-tags and empty-element tags (but not end-tags) may also have *attributes*. (In Example 1-2, the `title` on the <card> tag and the `src` on the <img> tag are both attributes.) Attributes affect the behavior of the whole element, which is why they can't appear on end-tags (the only purpose of the end-tag is to mark the end of the element). The effects of attributes vary between different elements: the `title` attribute on the <card> element sets an optional title to be displayed with the card, while the `src` attribute on the <img> element gives the URL at which the

---

* Again, you may recognize this as another feature WML takes from XML. This feature is critical to XML, and it also makes WML files easier for the browser to read and parse. If you don't know XML, don't worry: just remember to add the extra slash whenever there isn't a matching end-tag.

† Looking at the document in terms of elements also comes from XML.

image can be found. You can also add an `align="center"` attribute to the `<p>` element, which centers that paragraph of text (if the browser supports the feature).

A further slight difference between WML and HTML is in the quoting of attribute *values*. In HTML, attribute values may appear in single quotes (`attr='value'`), in double quotes (`attr="value"`), and most web browsers also allow them to be unquoted altogether (`attr=value`), although this isn't strictly valid. WML doesn't allow unquoted attribute values: all values must appear within either single or double quotes.*

Notation for Attributes

Within this book, whenever an attribute is described, a brief summary of the type of value it takes is given in parentheses after its name. The following terms are used in these descriptions:

string
> The value can be any string.

url
> The value should be a valid URL. Unless noted otherwise in the description of the attribute, *relative* URLs (where only part of the URL is given) are OK; these are resolved relative to the current document's URL. *Resolving* is the process of taking an incomplete (relative) URL and turning it into a complete (absolute) URL. It is described in detail in Appendix A, *Absolute and Relative URLs*.

number
> The value should be a nonnegative integer.

length
> The value represents a length on the browser's display. It can be specified either as a whole number of pixels or as a percentage (which represents a percentage of the width or height of the screen). In either case, the value must not be negative (but may be zero).

boolean
> The value should be one of the strings `true` or `false`. Case is important!

name
> The value should be a string containing only letters, digits, dots, colons, hyphens, and underscores. It is better, however, to avoid the dots, colons, and hyphens, and use only letters, digits, and underscores.

---

* The rules for quoting attribute values are another thing that will be familiar to XML users, since WML takes them from XML. If you don't know XML, just remember you must use either single or double quotes around all attribute values.

variable

> The value may contain embedded variable references (see Chapter 2, *WML Variables and Contexts*, for more information on variables).

optional

> The attribute may be omitted.

required

> The attribute must be present for the element to be processed correctly. Many browsers will refuse to process a deck if required attributes are missing.

default

> The default value for the attribute. This value is used if the attribute isn't specified on the tag. Only optional attributes can have defaults.

Entities

The final bit of WML syntax you need before starting on the range of different elements is the *entity*. You may recognize entities if you've ever had to put certain special symbols (quotes, greater than and less than signs, and several others) into an HTML page. Their purpose is to represent symbols that either can't easily be typed in (you may not have a British pound sign on your keyboard) or that have a special meaning in WML. (For example, if you put a < character into your text normally, the browser thinks it's the start of a tag; the browser then complains when it can't find the matching > character to end the tag.)

Table 1-1 displays the three forms of entities in WML. Named entities are something you may be familiar with from HTML: they look like & or <, and they represent a single named character via a mnemonic name. Entities can also be entered in one of two numeric forms (decimal or hexadecimal), allowing you to enter any Unicode character into your WML. (This doesn't guarantee that the browser can display it, but at least you can try.) Decimal numeric entities look like ! (Unicode exclamation mark) or £ (Unicode pound sign). Hexadecimal numeric entities look like ! or £ for the same two characters (note that 33 decimal is 21 hexadecimal, and 163 decimal is A3 hexadecimal).

Table 1-1. Named Entities and Their Equivalents

Named Entity	Decimal Entity	Hexadecimal Entity	Character
&quot;	&#34;	&#x22;	Double quote (")
&amp;	&#38;	&#x26;	Ampersand (&)
&apos;	&#39;	&#x27;	Apostrophe (')
&lt;	&#60;	&#x3C;	Less than (<)
&gt;	&#62;	&#x3E;	Greater than (>)

Table 1-1. Named Entities and Their Equivalents (continued)

Named Entity	Decimal Entity	Hexadecimal Entity	Character
			Nonbreaking space
&shy;	&#173;	&#xAD;	Soft hyphen

Note that all entities start with an ampersand (&) and end with a semicolon (;). This semicolon is very important: some web pages forget this and cause problems for browsers that want correct HTML (most web browsers are forgiving about slightly incorrect HTML syntax, so many common errors slip through). WAP browsers are likely to be stricter about errors like these.

The last two entities in the table may require some explanation. When the browser needs to break a long line of text in order to fit it onto the screen, it looks for a suitable point at which to break, such as the gap between two words. Normally, this means that lines are broken at spaces.

A *nonbreaking space* is a special kind of space that doesn't mark a word boundary, and so the browser doesn't break the line there. Nonbreaking spaces are useful when the characters surrounding the space are not normal English text. In some computer typesetting systems, they are also used to make the line breaks in long passages of text fall in places that make the text easier to read, but this is unlikely to be of use with WAP.

Soft hyphens are also linked to line breaking, but instead of preventing a break, they mark a place in a long word where a break is permissible (a *discretionary hyphen* in computer-typesetting parlance). The hyphen is displayed only if the line is broken at that point.[*]

Comments

Sometimes you may find that you want to leave a remark in your WML file to remind you how it works at some later date, or you may want to temporarily remove part of a file while you are testing something else. *Comments* are the answer.

A comment starts with the four characters `<!--` and ends with the three characters `-->`. Everything that appears between these two markers, including tags, body text, entities, and line breaks, is ignored. Here are some examples:

---

[*] Entities and their different forms are yet another XML feature in WML, although XML allows them to be more complicated than this (you really don't want to know). HTML users may know that there are many more entities available in HTML, such as `&copy;` for a copyright symbol, but WML requires that any beyond the few provided be entered using the numeric forms.

```
<!-- A simple comment. -->

<!--This is
a comment that
spans several lines.-->
```

You can't nest comments. The following doesn't work:

```
<!-- A simple <!-- EMBEDDED COMMENT, NOT! -->   comment. -->
```

Moreover, the two characters `--` can't appear within the body of a comment, only at the end, as part of the `-->` terminator.

If for some reason you want the sequence `<!--` in your body text, write it with an entity (which you would have to do for the `<` anyway):

```
&lt;!--
```

You may be worrying about using comments. Surely they end up sending lots of extra data to the browser, and you keep being told how saving bandwidth is really important? Don't worry: the WAP gateway removes all comments as part of its processing, so the browser doesn't even know they exist.

2

WML Variables and Contexts

A significant difference between WML and HTML is that WML supports *variables*. WML variables contain strings, and these strings can be inserted into the body text of the WML document or into the values of certain attributes. The values of variables can be changed under the control of the WML itself and also from within WMLScript functions (more on these later).

The names of WML variables can consist of any combination of letters, digits, and underscores, except that the first character must not be a digit. Like most things in WML, variable names are case-sensitive. The following are all examples of legal variable names:

```
a
foo
__name_with_underscores__
ThisVariableNameIsImpracticalBecauseItIsTooLong
xy17
```

The following are examples of invalid variable names:

```
17xy              (starts with a digit)
name with spaces  (space is not a letter, digit, or underscore)
```

Although WML doesn't impose a limit on the length of variable names, remember that the full name needs to be transmitted over a low-bandwidth link and then stored in the (possibly limited) memory on the device running the browser. As a result, it's a good idea to keep your variable names short.

Variable Substitution

Variables can be inserted (or *substituted*) into the body text or an attribute value in one of three ways:

```
$name
$(name)
$(name:conversion)
```

If the first form is used, the variable name must be followed by some character that's illegal in variable names (any character other than a letter, digit, or underscore).

 Because of this, it is unwise to use the first form: not only is it less clear than the second, it can also be dangerous, as a minor change to the file (such as removing a space) can change what the browser believes the variable name to be. In addition, some current browsers don't support this form properly.

The conversion specified with the third form can take one of three values, each of which can also be abbreviated to its first letter. Unusually for WML, these conversion specifiers are case-insensitive:

escape *or* e

> The variable's value undergoes *URL escaping* before it is substituted. This process replaces certain characters in the value with an *escape sequence*, consisting of a % followed by two hexadecimal digits. In addition, each space character in the value is replaced by a +.
>
> For example, if the value of the variable NickNames is Buz, Rocket, then $(NickNames:e) is replaced by Buz%2C+Rocket. (The hexadecimal code for the comma (,) character is 2C.)
>
> Note that even though this process is called URL escaping, the value doesn't have to be a URL: any string can be used.

unesc *or* u

> The variable's value undergoes the inverse of URL escaping, known as *URL unescaping*. This process reverses the steps involved in URL escaping: it replaces sequences of a % and two hexadecimal digits with single characters and each + with a space.
>
> For example, if the value of the variable NickNamesE is Buz%2C+Rocket, then $(NickNamesE:u) is replaced by Buz, Rocket. (Note that this has exactly reversed the previous example.)

`noesc` *or* n

The value is substituted directly. No conversion is done.

If there is no *conversion* specified ($*name* or $(*name*) forms), the browser performs a default conversion. This default depends on the context of the reference. If the variable is being substituted into an attribute of type `onenterforward`, `onenterbackward`, `href`, or `src`, then the conversion defaults to `escape`, because all these attribute values specify URLs to various things (you'll learn about these in later chapters). In all other contexts (including all substitutions into the body text), the default is `noesc`.

A point to bear in mind (after you've read Chapter 3, *WML Tasks and Events*, and Chapter 7, *WML Text and Text Formatting*) is that attributes of types `onclick` and `ontimer` default to `noesc`, although you might expect them to default to `escape` like `onenterforward` and `onenterbackward` do. Because of these inconsistencies, wise WAP developers always specify a conversion explicitly (even if the conversion is `noesc`) when substituting variables into attribute values, particularly when those values store URLs.

To illustrate these conversions, suppose the variable `user` contains the value `fred`, and `greeting` contains `Hello, world!`. Then the attribute:

```
title="Welcome, $(user)! $(greeting)"
```

becomes:

```
title="Welcome, fred! Hello, world!"
```

Similarly, the attribute:

```
href="/cgi-bin/login?u=$(user)&amp;g=$(greeting)"
```

is equivalent (because the default conversion of variables within an `href` attribute is `escape`) to:

```
href="/cgi-bin/login?u=$(user:e)&amp;g=$(greeting:e)"
```

which then becomes:

```
href="/cgi-bin/login?u=fred&amp;g=Hello%2C+world%21"
```

once variables are substituted. Note that this last example would have been better written using its more explicit form (using `:e`), rather than relying on the browser to perform default conversion.

Note also the use of `&amp;` to include a & in the URL value. A common mistake (and one that even experienced developers make from time to time) is to write just & and then spend hours trying to figure out why it doesn't work properly.

Empty Variables

You may wonder what happens if you try to substitute a variable that has not been defined: does it cause an error? Does anything happen at all?

The simple answer is that any undefined variable is equivalent to the empty string, so:

```
foo$(undefined)bar
```

becomes:

```
foobar
```

after variable substitution. In addition, assigning the empty string to a variable removes it from the browser context (see the section "Browser Contexts" later in this chapter).

Caveats of Variable Substitution

You may be wondering how, if a $ starts a variable, you can put a literal $ into the page or an attribute value. For example, you may want to display the string:

```
Price: $17.00
```

You may think that entities are the answer: maybe you could just put in $ to make it work. Unfortunately, it doesn't, due to the way WML browsers handle variable substitution.

What happens is that the browser goes through the document replacing all the entities with the characters they represent, before it even starts to look for variable references. While $ does indeed represent a $, the browser then interprets this $ as the start of a variable reference, which is exactly what you don't want to happen! (See the sidebar, "WML Variables and XML," for a further discussion.)

Fortunately, there is a way out. The sequence $$ always represents a single $ when it appears in body text or attribute values. Thus the correct way to display the string `Price: $17.00` is:

```
Price: $$17.00
```

This also means that the sequence $$(foo) represents the six characters $(foo) and not any sort of variable reference. The sequence $$$(foo) represents the character $ followed by the contents of variable foo with the default conversion. A single $ by itself (not followed by another $, a (, or the start of a variable name) is illegal.

WML Variables and XML

The reason you can't work around WML variables with entities lies with the relationship between WML and XML.

WML is designed so that a generic XML parser can process the page. The parser takes the source file and make a single pass over it, turning all the elements into a tree structure, with the body text interspersed. Entities are expanded in the same single pass, so that the body text in the tree doesn't contain any special XML syntax: it is just simple text.

XML doesn't treat WML variables specially; at this point the sequence $(foo) is just a six-character string.

Only after this XML-level parsing is complete does the WML parser get to see the page and handle WML variables. By this time, all $ entities have become simple $ characters, which the WML parser considers to be the start of a variable reference.

This situation also explains why you can't change the page structure with variables: the structure of the page is defined at the XML level using tags and attributes; WML variables are handled later. If the XML parser finds a $ character in a tag or attribute name, it simply rejects the document. $ isn't a legal name character in an XML name.

 It's necessary to write a single $ as $$ even in attribute values that don't allow variables. This is because the browser checks all attribute values for variables, even if there shouldn't be any variables there, and will probably complain if it finds any in the wrong place.

Another thing to watch out for is that you can't change the actual structure of the page using variables. You can change text in between tags, and you can change some attribute values, but you can't add any new tags or attributes.

If the variable `img` contains the value `<img src="img.wbmp"/>`, then the text:

    some text$(img)some more text

is simply equivalent to the string:

    some text<img src="img.wbmp"/>some more text

and *not* to two separate strings with an image in between.

The following tags are both illegal no matter what the value of the foo variable is:

```
<$(foo) href="img.wbmp"/>
<img $(foo)="img.wbmp"/>
```

If you really need to make changes to the structure of the page like that, you have to do it on the server.

Setting Variables

You now know just about everything there is to know about actually using WML variables, but one thing you don't yet know is how to put useful values into the variables in the first place!

Actually, there are three ways. The most common is through the use of the various user interface elements, which are described in Chapter 4, *WML User Interaction*. Variables can also be set from WMLScript, as explained in Chapter 19, *The WMLBrowser Library*. The third way is with the <setvar> element.

The <setvar> Element

This element must be placed within a *task* element (described in Chapter 3). Its purpose is to represent an assignment to a WML variable. This assignment takes place when the task is executed.

Attributes of the <setvar> element

name *(required; variable string)*
   Specifies the name of the variable to be set

value *(required; variable string)*
   Specifies the new value for the variable

For example, the element:

```
<setvar name="var" value="foo"/>
```

creates a variable called var, containing the string foo. If a variable called var already exists, this changes its value to the string foo.

Order of Operations in Setting Variables

Before executing one or more <setvar> elements within a task, the browser first expands all variables in all the name and value attributes. Note that this makes the order of the <setvar> elements within a task unimportant.

To illustrate this behavior, imagine that the variable x contains the value one, y contains two, and z contains three. Now suppose a task contains these three `<setvar>` elements:

```
<setvar name="x" value="$(y)"/>
<setvar name="y" value="$(z)"/>
<setvar name="z" value="$(x)"/>
```

The browser first substitutes all the variables:

```
<setvar name="x" value="two"/>
<setvar name="y" value="three"/>
<setvar name="z" value="one"/>
```

Finally, the browser assigns the new values to the three variables.

Note that this principle of substituting variables first extends to both the name and value attributes of the `<setvar>` element. For example, if the variable category has the value color, and variable choice has the value green, then:

```
<setvar name="$(category)" value="$(choice)"/>
```

becomes:

```
<setvar name="color" value="green"/>
```

This form (with variables in the name) isn't used often, but it's worth knowing that it exists.

Browser Contexts

The *browser context* in WML is the set of all variables currently set, together with the *history stack* (the list of all the cards the user has recently visited).

The context is emptied (all variables are unset, and the stack is emptied) when a card is displayed with the newcontext attribute set to true. See Chapter 6, *WML Decks, Templates, and Cards,* for more on cards and their attributes.

In addition, whenever the user sends the browser to a new location that wasn't referenced in the current card (for example, by selecting a bookmark, entering a new URL, or viewing an initial home card), a new context is created. Some browsers support multiple contexts, in which case it may be possible to get back to the previous context somehow. But many support only one, meaning that this is equivalent to emptying the context permanently. This new context action doesn't happen if the new URL came from executing a task, only if it came from some external source.

3

WML Tasks and Events

In the last chapter, you learned about variables in WML, something not found in HTML. This chapter covers two further parts of WML—tasks and events—that have no real equivalent in HTML. (In some cases you can use JavaScript to achieve similar effects.)

Tasks

A WML *task* is an element that specifies an action to be performed by the browser, rather than something to be displayed. For example, the action of changing to a new card is represented by a <go> task element, and the action of returning to the previous card visited is represented by a <prev> task element. Task elements encapsulate all the information required to perform the action.

Tasks are used in many places in WML. *Events* (discussed later in this chapter) are tied closely with tasks, and many of the user interface elements (see Chapter 4, *WML User Interaction*) use tasks to perform actions.

To see how tasks are used in context, consider the element <do>, which represents some sort of control that the user can activate, such as a softkey, a menu item on a cell phone, or maybe even an onscreen button if the device has a touchscreen. A <do> element isn't itself a task element. Rather, it contains a task subelement that specifies the action to perform when the user activates the control.

A <do> element that, on activation, simply assigns the value **wibble** to the variable **test** can be written as:

```
<do type="accept">
    <refresh>
        <setvar name="test" value="wibble"/>
```

```
    </refresh>
  </do>
```

To have the same `<do>` element instead send the browser to a card called `card2` in the current deck, you could write:

```
<do type="accept">
    <go href="#card2"/>
</do>
```

Note that the `<do>` element is exactly the same for these two examples. The only difference is the task element (the `<refresh>` or the `<go>`). This added consistency (or *orthogonality* to use the technical term) is an important benefit of using tasks.

The `<do>` element is explained more fully in Chapter 4.

Tasks and Variables

All tasks can change variables in the browser's context using the `<setvar>` element, as described in Chapter 2, *WML Variables and Contexts*. The new variable bindings don't affect the task itself but rather take effect when the task completes. For example, suppose the variable `page` contains the value `login`. The task:

```
<go href="$(page).wml">
    <setvar name="page" value="bad"/>
</go>
```

goes to `login.wml`, not `bad.wml`, because the browser substitutes the original value of the `page` variable into the `href` attribute before it assigns the new value to the variable.

The `<go>` Task

As the name suggests, the `<go>` task represents the action of going to a new card. (It is also used for a special purpose with WMLScript, but you must wait until later in the book to find out about that.)

The `<go>` task takes several different attributes to customize exactly how to find the new card. Usually, only `href` and sometimes `method` attributes are used.

Attributes of the `<go>` task

`href` *(required variable url)*

> Gives the URL of the new card. Relative URLs are resolved relative to the current card (the one containing this `<go>`).

method *(optional string; default* get*)*

> Specifies the method that should be used to fetch the deck. This must be one of the values get or post, corresponding to the GET and POST methods of HTTP.

sendreferer *(optional boolean; default* false*)*

> If set to true, the browser sends the URL of the current deck along with the request. This URL is sent as a relative URL if possible. The purpose of this is to allow servers to perform simple access control on decks, based on which decks are linking to them. For example, using HTTP, this attribute is sent in the HTTP Referer header.

accept-charset *(optional string; default* unknown*)*

> Specifies a comma- or space-separated list of character sets that can encode data sent to the server in a POST request. The browser selects one to use when sending the data. If this is set to the value unknown (the default), the browser uses the same character set that sent this document to the browser. (Note that this attribute is an advanced feature and is rarely used.)

The method attribute: GET and POST

One of the more interesting options available on the <go> task is the method attribute. This specifies whether the request should be sent as a GET or as a POST. This option is used only when sending information for processing on the server: it's not used when simply fetching static pages of WML.

If you know HTML, you may recognize similarities with the METHOD="GET" and METHOD="POST" attributes that can be put on an HTML <FORM> element. WML puts this attribute on the <go> task instead, but it has essentially the same effect.

GET is the normal method used in HTTP. All the information sent to the server is encoded in the URL, and the server uses this URL to find some resource and return it to the browser.

The main advantage of GET is that it's simple. Any information is simply added to the query part of the URL (more on the parts of URLs in Appendix A, *Absolute and Relative URLs*). You can even put the query information directly into the URL using variables.

The main disadvantage of GET is that it can be used only for a limited amount of data. Web servers and other programs that process URLs impose certain limits on the length of a URL they are prepared to handle. This limits the size of the request that can be sent using GET.

A subtler problem with GET relates to the fact that all the information you send becomes part of the URL. Many browsers display the URL of the current deck somewhere on the screen (even if only briefly), and most web servers store the entire URL in their log files, complete with the extra data from the GET. If this information is of a sensitive nature (a password, for example), it's displayed on the screen and then saved for posterity in the web server's logs!

The POST method avoids these two problems, by sending the data separately from the URL in the request. As a result, the URL stays small, and the browser display and web server logs don't contain any of the data.

The <postfield> element

In modern versions of WML, information to be posted with the POST method is specified in <postfield> elements within the <go> element. This information takes the form of a list of name/value pairs. Each <postfield> element specifies a single pair. The element is very simple, having only two attributes:

name *(required variable string)*
> The name of this field

value *(required variable string)*
> The value of this field

WML allows <postfield> elements to be used even with the GET method. In this case, the fields are added to the end of the query part of the URL. For example, consider the task:

```
<go href="wibble" method="get">
    <postfield name="x" value="17"/>
    <postfield name="y" value="42"/>
</go>
```

This has the same effect as:

```
<go href="wibble?x=17&amp;y=42" method="get"/>
```

Using the <postfield> element in this way can make your WML much clearer and also makes your life much easier if you have to change the WML to use POST at some point in the future.

You can even mix the two styles. Here's another way to write exactly the same <go> task as the last two examples:

```
<go href="wibble?x=17" method="get">
    <postfield name="y" value="42"/>
</go>
```

Shorthand forms of <go> tasks

One form of task is more common than any other: a <go> task that has no attributes other than href and doesn't contain any <postfield> or <setvar>

elements. Because this form is so common, WML provides a shorthand form you can use in many situations.

Instead of including the task as a complete `<go>` element, the value that would be put into the `href` attribute of the `<go>` element is simply included as an attribute on a different element. For example, it is possible to bind a task to an option in a selection list, so that the task is performed when the option is selected. The normal way of doing this looks like this:

```
<option>
    <onevent type="onpick">
        <go href="foo.wml"/>
    </onevent>
    Option text
<option>
```

Using the shorthand form, this can be written as:

```
<option onpick="foo.wml">
    Option text
</option>
```

I think you'll agree, that's much shorter and clearer.

This is allowed for the **onenterforward**, **onenterbackward**, and **ontimer** attributes of the `<card>` element; the **onpick** attribute of the `<option>` element; and the `href` attribute of the `<a>` element. These elements are all described later in this book: don't worry about them for now.

The <prev> Task

The `<prev>` task represents the action of returning to the previously visited card on the history stack. When this action is performed, the top entry is removed from the history stack, and that card is displayed again, after any `<setvar>` variable assignments in the `<prev>` task have taken effect.

The `<prev>` task takes no attributes.

Most uses of the `<prev>` task are very simple. Usually no variables are involved, and so most `<prev>` tasks are simply:

```
<prev/>
```

A `<prev>` task is most commonly used in connection with a `<do>` element (described in Chapter 4). Some browsers don't provide a back button unless one is specified in the WML, and so a great deal of WML contains the construct:

```
<do type="prev"><prev/></do>
```

This simply provides a button or some other user-interface construct, which when activated, sends the browser to the previous card.

One situation where it can be useful to include variables in a `<prev>` task is a login page, which prompts for a username and password. In some situations, you may want to clear out the password field when returning to the login card, forcing the user to reenter it. This can be done with a construct such as:

```
<prev>
    <setvar name="password" value=""/>
</prev>
```

The <refresh> Task

The `<refresh>` task is the simplest task that actually does something. Its effect is simply to perform the variable assignments specified by its `<setvar>` elements, then redisplay the current card with the new values. The `<go>` and `<prev>` tasks perform the same action just before displaying the new card.

The `<refresh>` task doesn't take any attributes.

The `<refresh>` task is most often used to perform some sort of "reset" action on the card. Example 3-1 shows how this could be done. The `<input>` elements prompt the user to enter strings and then store the strings into the variables specified in their **name** attributes (see Chapter 4 for more information). There is also a `<go>` task using the POST method to submit the login and password information to a server for processing.

Example 3-1. A Reset Button

```
<?xml version="1.0"?>
<!DOCTYPE wml PUBLIC
    "-//WAPFORUM//DTD WML 1.1//EN"
    "http://www.wapforum.org/DTD/wml_1.1.xml">

<wml>
    <card title="Reset button example">
        <!-- Read login and password from user. -->
        <p>Login:    <input name="login"/></p>
        <p>Password: <input name="password"/></p>

        <!-- Submit button sends data to server. -->
        <do type="accept" label="Submit">
            <go href="login.cgi" method="post">
                <postfield name="l" value="$(login)"/>
                <postfield name="p" value="$(password)"/>
            </go>
        </do>

        <!-- Reset button clears login and password. -->
        <do type="reset" label="Reset">
            <refresh>
                <setvar name="login" value=""/>
                <setvar name="password" value=""/>
            </refresh>
```

Example 3-1. A Reset Button (continued)

```
        </do>
    </card>
</wml>
```

The <noop> Task

The purpose of the <noop> task is to do nothing (no operation). This may seem particularly useless: why would anyone want a task that doesn't do anything?

The only real use for this task is in connection with *templates* (discussed in more detail in Chapter 6, *WML Decks, Templates, and Cards*). However, it can also be specified anywhere a task is required.

The <noop> task is the only exception to the rule that tasks can set variables. It can't set variables and can't even contain any <setvar> elements. If you want a task to just set variables and not change the current card, use the <refresh> task.

The <noop> task doesn't take any attributes.

Because the <noop> task takes no attributes and can't even contain any <setvar> elements, it always looks the same in use:

```
<noop/>
```

Events

An *event* in WML is simply something that can happen to some element from time to time. For example, entering a <card> element triggers an event on the <card>, and selecting an <option> from a selection list triggers an event on the <option>.

You can harness these events by *binding* them to a task. The usual way of doing this is with the <onevent> element. As mentioned earlier in this chapter, for simple <go> tasks you can usually make use of a simpler form: this will be mentioned when when we discuss the elements in question.

For example, the <option> element (detailed in Chapter 4) declares an item in a list of selections. When this item is selected, it triggers an onpick event on the <option> element. Suppose the element were declared without an event handler, like this:

```
<option>
    Purple
</option>
```

In this case, the `onpick` event is ignored, since there is no handler. If, on the other hand, the option is declared as:

```
<option>
    <onevent type="onpick">
        <go href="#purple"/>
    </onevent>

    Purple
</option>
```

the `onpick` event is handled by executing the `<go>` task, sending the browser to a new card.

The <onevent> Element

The `<onevent>` element declares an event binding. It can't contain anything except a single task element that is performed when the event occurs. It may be present inside either an `<option>` element (see Chapter 4) or a `<card>` element (see Chapter 6). In either case, the `<onevent>` element (or elements) must be the first elements declared inside their enclosing element.

The `<onevent>` element takes only one attribute:

type *(required string)*
   Gives the type of event to which the task should be bound. For example, use `type="ontimer"` to bind to the `ontimer` event of a `<card>` element.

Card Events

Sometimes, you may want to do something special when the user enters a particular card. For example, you may want to initialize the values of variables so that the display looks correct. Another thing you may want to do is to clear out some variables when the user returns to a particular card in the history stack.

To make this possible, WML defines two events, **onenterforward** and **onenterbackward**, which happen on a `<card>` element when the user enters it. Which event occurs depends on how the card was entered.

The onenterforward event

The **onenterforward** event occurs when a card is entered in the forward direction. Entering as a result of a `<go>` task, selecting a bookmark, or entering a URL directly are all in the forward direction. The most common use of this event is to initialize things that must be set up before the card is displayed, often by using a `<refresh>` task or by using a `<go>` task to run some WMLScript (see "Calling WMLScript from WML" in Chapter 13, *WMLScript Functions*).

Example 3-2 shows how this can be used. When the first card is entered forwards, the <refresh> task is performed, which initializes the **state** variable. This variable can then be updated by other WML pages and is passed through to the server by the <go> task.

Example 3-2. Initialization on Entry

```
<?xml version="1.0"?>
<!DOCTYPE wml PUBLIC
    "-//WAPFORUM//DTD WML 1.1//EN"
    "http://www.wapforum.org/DTD/wml_1.1.xml">

<wml>
    <card title="onenterforward example">
        <!-- Initialize state to zero on first entry. -->
        <onevent type="onenterforward">
            <refresh>
                <setvar name="state" value="0"/>
            </refresh>
        </onevent>

        <!-- Collect some information from the user. -->
        <p><input name="text"/></p>

        <!-- Send the text and the state to the server. -->
        <do type="accept">
            <go href="submit.cgi">
                <postfield name="s" value="$(state)"/>
                <postfield name="t" value="$(text)"/>
            </go>
        </do>
    </card>
</wml>
```

If the task bound to the **onenterforward** event is a simple <go> task without <setvar> or <postfield> elements, you can use the shorthand form introduced earlier in this chapter: just add an **onenterforward** attribute to the <card> element. The value of this attribute is the destination URL.

For example, the event binding:

```
<card title="example">
    <onevent type="onenterforward">
        <go href="#card2"/>
    <onevent>

    <!-- rest of card -->
</card>
```

is equivalent to the shorter form:

```
<card title="example" onenterforward="#card2">
    <!-- rest of card -->
</card>
```

It's your choice to use the shorthand form, but it means less typing and results in less data being sent to the browser.

Be warned that not all tasks you can bind to the `onenterforward` event actually make sense. For example, the event binding:

```
<onevent type="onenterforward">
    <prev/>
</onevent>
```

makes it impossible for the user to enter the card at all: as soon as she went to the card, the browser would immediately return to the previous one!

To make matters worse, the event binding:

```
<card id="card1" onenterforward="#card1">
```

means that as soon as the browser entered the card, it would be immediately redirected to the same card, which would cause an immediate redirect to the same card, and again, and again. . . . Well-written browsers may notice this and signal an error, but not all browsers are well-written: many simply lock up or even crash.

The onenterbackward event

The `onenterbackward` event is the companion of the `onenterforward` event for the backward direction. This event is triggered when the card is returned to as the result of a `<prev>` task or some other action that navigates backwards in the history stack.

The most common use for the `onenterbackward` event is to reset state back to some initial value when returning to the beginning. Example 3-3 alters Example 3-1 to illustrate this: instead of an explicit reset button, the login and password are cleared when the user returns to this card via the history stack.

Example 3-3. Reset on Reentry

```
<?xml version="1.0"?>
<!DOCTYPE wml PUBLIC
    "-//WAPFORUM//DTD WML 1.1//EN"
    "http://www.wapforum.org/DTD/wml_1.1.xml">

<wml>
    <card title="Reset on reentry example">
        <!-- Reset fields when entered backwards. -->
        <onevent type="onenterbackward">
            <refresh>
                <setvar name="login" value=""/>
                <setvar name="password" value=""/>
            </refresh>
        </onevent>
```

Example 3-3. Reset on Reentry (continued)

```
        <!-- Read login and password from user. -->
        <p>Login:    <input name="login"/></p>
        <p>Password: <input name="password"/></p>

        <!-- Submit button sends data to server. -->
        <do type="accept" label="Submit">
            <go href="login.cgi" method="post">
                <postfield name="l" value="$(login)"/>
                <postfield name="p" value="$(password)"/>
            </go>
        </do>
    </card>
</wml>
```

Just as with the **onenterforward** event, **onenterbackward** also has a shorthand form in the case where the task is a simple form of **<go>**, meaning that the event binding:

```
<card title="example">
    <onevent type="onenterbackward">
        <go href="foo.wml"/>
    </onevent>

    <!-- rest of card -->
</card>
```

is equivalent to:

```
<card title="example" onenterbackward="foo.wml">
    <!-- rest of card -->
</card>
```

4

WML User Interaction

The previous two chapters described some of the features found in WML that don't exist in HTML. This chapter covers the features that WML provides to receive input from the user, and most of these are much more powerful than their equivalents in HTML.

The main reason for this extra power is that WML has variables. In HTML, you can have controls such as pulldown menus or text input fields, but you can use these in only limited ways: in an HTML *form*, which allows you to collect a number of controls and send their results to a server for processing, or with Java or JavaScript, which are complete programming languages built into the web browser.

Problems with Web Interaction

Using HTML forms for this purpose suffers from one major problem: the processing has to be done on the server. The client displays the controls, collects their results, packages them, and sends them to the server, but that's it. Apart from some simple constraints such as the maximum length of the text in an input box, you can't even check the input for validity before sending it off. This results in a lot of extra network connections, slowing things down a lot, even on a fast Internet link. Imagine how slow all those extra network connections are on a much slower link, as WAP has to contend with.

Using Java or JavaScript to collect the input does allow local processing, but they come complete with their own sets of problems. For a start, they both require a lot more from the browser: most older browsers have either no support for these or very limited or buggy support, which makes it harder to write pages that work across all browsers. Most text-only browsers don't support these at all. (Yes, some people do still use text-only browsers.)

Another, subtler problem with the Web's way of doing these things is that there are multiple ways to declare the controls. Suppose you want to display a text input box. Using a form, you can use something like:

```
<INPUT TYPE="TEXT" NAME="wibble">
```

Using JavaScript with the HTML, possibly:

```
<INPUT TYPE="TEXT" NAME="wibble" ONCHANGE="wibble_chg();">
```

If using Java applets, something like:*

```
TextField wibble = new TextField ();
add (wibble);
```

Each of these fragments has to be referenced in a completely different way from within the HTML page that forms the skeleton. Furthermore, the same control has to be added to the page in three different ways, even though they are all drawn in the same way by the browser, and the user interacts with each in the same way. This makes it hard to change the action of a control once it has been implemented. It requires rewriting everything related to that control, and probably restructuring the whole page as well.

Interaction in WAP

For comparison, here is how the same text input box is described in WML, where its result is sent directly to the server:

```
<input name="wibble"/>
```

Here, its result is passed to some WMLScript to check it for validity before passing it to the server:

```
<input name="wibble"/>
```

Here, it's displayed to the user in another card for confirmation purposes, without any server transactions involved:

```
<input name="wibble"/>
```

These three examples are identical because the same control is always written in the same way in WML. Doing it this way works because none of the controls ever perform any direct action. They are instead linked to the lower-level layers of WML, such as variables and tasks.

---

* It isn't completely fair to compare Java with HTML here, since Java is a full-featured programming language, and HTML is just a markup language. But since Java is often used to implement this sort of thing on web pages, it's appropriate to mention it here.

For example, in the previous <input> element, the only effect of the user enter-ing some text into the box is that the variable **wibble** is set to a new value. The browser doesn't directly send the text to the server or call any scripts: it's up to you to use the value of this variable at some point.

The <input> Element

Let's start our exploration of WML's mechanisms for user interaction with the <input> element, since we've just seen it in action.

This element is used whenever the user needs to enter a string or some other piece of text. Usually, this should be kept as short as possible, since many WAP users use cell phone keypads to enter these. Entering the letter **S** on a computer keyboard is easy, but this requires four keypresses on most cell phones. Symbols are even worse: with the exception of a few, such as **.** and **+**, symbols are very time-consuming to enter.

The <input> element can also be used to enter passwords or other sensitive information. In these cases, the element can be configured to not display the text as it's being entered. (In the case of cell phones, most display each character for a short time but then replace it with a ***** or other symbol.)

This element is also used for entering numbers. In cases like this, where the range of characters is restricted, it's possible to set a *format* for the string, which may speed up input. To do so, set the format to allow only digits; a cell phone knows that the keys don't need to cycle through all the letters before offering a digit (the digits are accessed with a single keypress instead of four or more).

This element (as with all user interaction elements) may be put anywhere in nor-mal paragraph text (namely, inside a <p> element). It takes nine[*] attributes, most of which are optional.

Attributes of the <input> Element

name *(required name)*

> Gives the name of the variable that gets the text from this element. When the element is displayed, it's initialized to the contents of this variable if it's set. If

---

[*] Strictly speaking, all WML elements may have three standard attributes, id, class, and xml:lang. Apart from one special use of the id attribute on the <card> element, the id and class attributes are intended for use in server-side applications, are ignored by the browser, and won't be mentioned again. The xml:lang attribute specifies "the natural or formal language" (to quote from the WML specification) of the element: its content is an abbreviation for a particular language (such as en for generic English). This is supposed to influence the display of the elements contained within (for example, certain lan-guages are written right to left rather than left to right), but it's not implemented by any current brows-ers, and hence won't be mentioned again. If this all sounds confusing, just forget it: everyone else does.

it isn't, the element is initialized to the value of the `value` attribute if present; otherwise it's initially empty.

`type` *(optional string; default* `text`*)*

If omitted or set to `text`, indicates that this element doesn't receive sensitive data, and that the text should be displayed as normal. If set to `password`, specifies that the text should be obscured in some way. This is normally done by replacing all the characters with some fixed character when displaying the contents. Any other value is illegal.

`value` *(optional variable string; default empty)*

Gives an optional initial value for the text in the element. This default is used only when the variable given by the `name` attribute isn't set. If that variable contains a value, its value initializes the element instead.

`format` *(optional string; default* `*M`*)*

Gives an optional format for the value. This format can display static text in the input area and can restrict the range of characters that may be entered. A smart browser uses this attribute to speed user input. A `format` attribute containing illegal codes is ignored. The legal codes are:

A   Any uppercase letter or symbol (not a digit).

a   Any lowercase letter or symbol (not a digit).

N   Any numeric character (digit or decimal points).

X   Any uppercase character.

x   Any lowercase character.

M   Any character: uppercase characters may be offered first, but anything is permitted.

m   Any character: lowercase characters may be offered first, but anything is permitted.

*f   Any number of characters (zero or more) matching format code *f* (where *f* is one of the previous format codes: A, a, N, X, x, M, or m). This may be specified only once and must be at the end of the string.

nf   Entry of exactly *n* characters (where *n* is a digit from 1 to 9), each matching format code *f*. This may be specified only once and must be at the end of the string. This is equivalent to using *n* occurrences of code *f*.

\c   Forces character *c* to be displayed in the text entry field. This character is displayed within the field and is passed through into the value.

For example, the format code `NNN\-NNNN` matches local North American telephone numbers (such as 555-1234).

Beware, however, of working too many assumptions such as this into your WAP decks, as different countries have different formats for things such as telephone numbers.

emptyok *(optional boolean; default* `false`*)*

If set to `true`, specifies that an empty string is a valid input, even if the `format` attribute otherwise prevents this. If the `format` string allows an empty input, that takes precedence, and `emptyok` is ignored. Since the default value for `format` allows empty input anyway, this attribute has no effect if no `format` attribute is given.

size *(optional number)*

Provides a hint as to how many characters wide the text input should be drawn, if the browser supports it (if it doesn't, this is ignored). This value doesn't limit the number of characters that can be entered into the element; for that, see the `maxlength` attribute.

maxlength *(optional number; default unlimited)*

Specifies the maximum number of characters that may be entered into this element.

title *(optional variable string)*

Gives a title to this element, which some browsers may use in its presentation.

tabindex *(optional number)*

Provides a hint to the browser about the order in which the user should be allowed to cycle through the elements. This attribute is described fully in the section "The tabindex Attribute" later in this chapter.

Examples of the <input> Element

Example 4-1 shows how a typical login page asking for a username and password can be constructed. The username is forced to consist entirely of lowercase letters, and the password is obscured when it's entered. Then there is a <do> element (explained later in this chapter), containing a <go> task. The effect of these last two is to add a button or similar control to the card, which sends the browser to the URL from the `href` attribute of the go task when it's activated.

Example 4-1. A Login Page

```
<?xml version="1.0"?>
<!DOCTYPE wml PUBLIC
    "-//WAPFORUM//DTD WML 1.1//EN"
    "http://www.wapforum.org/DTD/wml_1.1.xml">
```

Example 4-1. A Login Page (continued)

```
<wml>
    <card title="Login">
        <p>Username:
            <input name="user" format="*x"/></p>
        <p>Password:
            <input name="pass" type="password"/></p>
        <do type="accept" title="Log In">
            <go href="login?u=$(user:e)&amp;p=$(pass:e)"/>
        </do>
    </card>
</wml>
```

The <select> Element

The other high-level control that WML provides is one allowing selection from a list of items. This replaces many different types of control, such as scrolling select-able lists, pulldown menus, and lists of checkboxes.

In its simplest form, the `<select>` element provides an `iname` attribute giving a WML variable name. Inside the `<select>` is a list of `<option>` elements. Select-ing an option sets the `iname` variable to the index of that item within the `<select>`, starting from 1. For example:

```
<select iname="animal">
    <option>Lizard</option>
    <option>Spider</option>
    <option>Squid</option>
</select>
```

Selecting `Lizard` sets `animal` to 1, selecting `Spider` sets it to 2, and selecting `Squid` sets it to 3.

In a slightly more complex form, the `<select>` element has a `name` attribute rather than `iname`, and a list of `<option>` elements, each of which has a `value` attribute. Selecting one of these options sets the `name` variable to the contents of the option's `value` attribute. For example, a list allowing the user to select a London airport can be written as:

```
<select name="airport">
    <option value="LHR">London Heathrow</option>
    <option value="LGW">London Gatwick</option>
    <option value="STN">London Stansted</option>
    <option value="LCY">London City</option>
    <option value="LTN">London Luton</option>
</select>
```

Selecting an option sets `airport` to the corresponding three-letter airport code.

Attributes of the <select> Element

title *(optional variable string)*

Provides an optional title for the <select> element, which some browsers may use in its presentation. Others may ignore it.

iname *(optional name)*

Specifies a WML variable to be set to the index of the selected item. If this is specified and the variable is already set to an index value, it selects the default value. This takes precedence over ivalue, name, and value for determining the default value.

ivalue *(optional variable number)*

Specifies the index of the value that should be the default if the iname attribute isn't present or its variable isn't set. This takes precedence over name and value for setting the default.

name *(optional name)*

Specifies a WML variable to be set to the contents of the value attribute from the selected option. This may also be used to determine the default value. (The first <option> whose value matches the contents of this variable is selected but only if iname and ivalue have failed to select an item.) This takes precedence over only value.

value *(optional variable string)*

Specifies the default value of the <select>. The first item with a value attribute matching this is selected. This attribute is used only when iname, ivalue, or name haven't managed to select a default value.

multiple *(optional boolean; default* false*)*

If set to true, indicates that this <select> should allow more than one <option> to be active at a time. In this case, the behavior of the name, value, iname, and ivalue attributes changes slightly. (More on this in the section "Multiple Selection," later in this chapter).

tabindex *(optional number)*

As with <input>, this provides a hint to the browser as to how it should cycle through all the controls in the card. See the section "The tabindex Attribute" later in the chapter for more on tabindex.

Multiple Selection

When a <select> item has a multiple="true" attribute, it allows more than one item to be selected from the list simultaneously. Such a <select> treats the values of the name, value, iname, and ivalue attributes differently than normal. Instead of each representing a single item (either an index or something matching an option's **value**), each is treated as a list of values separated by semicolons. (This has the minor side-effect that semicolons are not valid in the **value** attributes on any **<option>** in a multiple-selection **<select>**.) The actual order of the values between the semicolons isn't defined by WML.

For example, a WAP pizza delivery service could use something similar to Example 4-2 to let people choose the toppings for their pizza. Note that this doesn't allow people to select the same topping more than once. If they want that, they can phone in the order!

Example 4-2. Multiple Selection

```
<?xml version="1.0"?>
<!DOCTYPE wml PUBLIC
    "-//WAPFORUM//DTD WML 1.1//EN"
    "http">

<wml>
    <card title="Pizza Toppings">
        <p>Choose your toppings:
        <select name="toppings" multiple="true">
            <option value="p">Pepperoni</option>
            <option value="h">Ham</option>
            <option value="b">Spicy Beef</option>
            <option value="a">Anchovies</option>
            <option value="c">Chillies</option>
            <option value="o">Olives</option>
            <option value="m">Mushrooms</option>
            <!-- ...lots more toppings here... -->
        </select></p>
        <do type="accept" label="Order">
            <go href="order?toppings=$(toppings:e)"/>
        </do>
    </card>
</wml>
```

If I then decide that I want a pizza with all these toppings except anchovies, the variable **toppings** is set to p;h;b;c;o;m, or m;o;c;b;h;p, or b;c;h;m;o;p, or any of the 717 other combinations of those six items. (No, I'm not going to list them all.)

If there had been an **iname** as well as (or perhaps instead of) the **name**, the variable it referenced is set to 1;2;3;5;6;7 or a permutation of those values.

In single-selection lists, however, the character ; is valid in option values. Example 4-3 shows Example 4-2 extended with an earlier card offering set pizzas and the chance to customize them by adding and removing toppings. Note that the option of going back from the second card to the first isn't provided here. This is because the values in the **toppings** variable may not be in the same order as

they were when the first **<select>** initialized them, because their order is not
fixed after a multiple selection.

Example 4-3. Mixed Selections

```
<?xml version="1.0"?>
<!DOCTYPE wml PUBLIC
    "-//WAPFORUM//DTD WML 1.1//EN"
    "http://www.wapforum.org/DTD/wml_1.1.xml">

<wml>
    <card title="Set Pizzas" id="pizzas">
        <p>Choose a Pizza:<select name="toppings">
            <option value="">
                <!-- no toppings -->
                Plain
            </option>
            <option value="p;m;o">
                <!-- pepperoni, mushrooms, olives -->
                Pepperoni Supreme
            </option>
            <option value="p;b;h;a;m;o;c">
                <!-- everything! -->
                Full House
            </option>
            <option value="c;o;m">
                <!-- chillies, olives, mushrooms -->
                Vegetarian
            </option>
        </select></p>
        <do type="accept" label="Order">
            <go href="order?toppings=$(toppings:e)"/>
        </do>
        <do type="accept" label="Customize">
            <go href="#toppings"/>
        </do>
    </card>

    <card title="Pizza Toppings" id="toppings">
        <p>Customize your Toppings
        <select name="toppings" multiple="true">
            <option value="p">Pepperoni</option>
            <option value="h">Ham</option>
            <option value="b">Spicy Beef</option>
            <option value="a">Anchovies</option>
            <option value="o">Olives</option>
            <option value="m">Mushrooms</option>
            <option value="c">Chillies</option>
        </select></p>
        <do type="accept" label="Order">
            <go href="order.cgi?toppings=$(toppings:e)"/>
        </do>
    </card>
</wml>
```

The <option> Element

While on the subject of the <select> element, it's time for a closer look at the <option> element that is so vital to it. You've already seen the two most common ways to use this element (with or without a value), but it's also possible to bind a task to an option, so that the task is performed when the user selects the option (or deselects it, for a multiple-selection list).

This task is bound to the onpick event. It can be bound either with a conventional <onevent> binding, or for simple <go> tasks it can be specified with the onpick attribute on the <option> tag itself.

Attributes of the <option> Element

value *(optional variable string)*
> Gives a value to this <option>, which is stored in the name variable of the <select>, as detailed earlier.

title *(optional variable string)*
> Gives a title to this <option>, which some browsers may use to display the option, but some may ignore.

onpick *(optional variable URL)*
> Provides a shorthand method of binding to the onpick event, for the common case where the task is a simple go. Because this task is reduced to just the URL, it cannot contain any <setvar> or <postfield> elements, and its method is limited to GET. In complicated cases, put an <onevent type="onpick"> element of type onpick inside the <option> element.

The <optgroup> Element

WAP doesn't define how the <select> element is displayed. It has been implemented in many different ways, including using pulldown menus, scrolling lists, and lines of checkboxes on PDA-type devices and several different types of menus on cell phones.

With a small screen, it isn't always possible to display all the available options at the same time. There are several ways to get around this problem: if the options are displayed normally in the text of the page, as with checkboxes for example, then the normal facilities for scrolling the page will do. Many cell phones simply display the currently selected option; activating this for editing changes the screen to a different display with the options. When the editing is complete, the display changes back to the card.

The purpose of the <optgroup> element is to divide a long list of options into several sections. Different browsers may use this information in different ways: many simply ignore it (particularly those running on devices with large screens). Others may display the title of the group as part of the option display but not do anything more with it. Some may use the group title as the name of a submenu, with the contents of the group in that submenu. The information is a hint, nothing more.

The <optgroup> element takes only one attribute:

title *(optional variable string)*
> Specifies a title for this group, which may be used by the browser (for example, as the title of a submenu). It may also be completely ignored.

As an example, the <optgroup> element can be used in the list of pizza toppings to separate the toppings into different groups:

```
<select name="toppings">
    <optgroup title="Meat &amp; Fish">
            <option value="p">Pepperoni</option>
            <option value="h">Ham</option>
            <option value="b">Spicy Beef</option>
            <option value="a">Anchovies</option>
    </optgroup>
    <optgroup title="Vegetables">
            <option value="o">Olives</option>
            <option value="m">Mushrooms</option>
            <option value="c">Chillies</option>
    </optgroup>
</select>
```

At publication time, few browsers support the <optgroup> element.

The <do> Element

The <input> and <select> elements provide high-level user controls, but sometimes all you want is a simple button or menu item. In these cases, the <do> element is exactly what you need.

A <do> element is simply a way to specify some arbitrary type of control for the browser to make available to the user. This can be rendered as a graphical button (as many PDA browsers do), as an item in a menu (as most cell phone browsers do), or as just about anything the user can know about and interact with. This can even include things such as voice commands for a hands-off WAP browser (in a car, for example).

A <do> element contains nothing but the task to be performed when the element is activated.

Attributes of the <do> Element

type *(required string)*

Specifies the type of this <do> element. This serves as a hint to the browser about the action this element triggers and may influence how the browser chooses to present the element. The following values are defined (undefined or unrecognized types are treated as if they had been specified as **unknown**):

accept

Acceptance of something. cell phones often bind this to the "yes" key if there is only one <do> of this type in the card.

prev

Navigation backwards in the history stack (a **<prev>** task or something similar).

help

Request for some sort of help. The help provided can be context-sensitive.

reset

An operation that clears or resets the state of the interaction; for example, a "clear and start over" operation on a group of text fields or an operation to deselect all options in a <select> element.

options

A context-sensitive request for additional options; for example, a button to bring up an "advanced options" menu.

delete

Delete a single item or choice. To delete all items, use the **reset** type instead.

unknown *(or empty string)*

A generic element that doesn't fit any existing category.

Any name starting with X- *or* x-

Experimental types. The exact behavior of these is undefined. Some browsers may implement some of these for development purposes. These types shouldn't be used in production systems.

Any name starting with vnd. *(case-insensitive)*

Vendor-specific types. Some browsers may implement specific <do> types of this form. Using these types allows you to enhance your WML for a specific browser, while remaining portable to others (unrecognized types are treated as if they were specified **unknown**).

label *(optional variable string)*

Specifies an optional text label for the element. For example, a browser that displays <do> elements as graphical buttons can use this as the button's text.

The WAP specifications recommend that to work well on the widest possible variety of browsers, this string should be limited to no more than six characters, but this rule isn't enforced.

name *(optional name)*

Specifies the name of this element, for the purposes of shadowing (see Chapter 6, *WML Decks, Templates, and Cards*, for more on shadowing). This type has no other effect.

optional *(optional boolean; default* false*)*

If set to true, informs the browser that it can ignore this <do> element.

The <anchor> Element

While the <do> element is useful, it isn't always what you want. Many cell phone browsers put all the <do> items in a card in a single menu, which means you can't guarantee it will appear where you want it to. Sometimes you want to make some of the text into an HTML-style link, rather than have a separate <do> control next to it. For example, if you have a menu of other pages available, you want the items in the menu to display in the correct order, as in Figure 4-1.

Almost all web pages use *hyperlinks*: text or images that can be activated to go to another page. Web browsers usually display these links underlined or in a different color so the user knows it's "clickable." These links are put into a web page with HTML's <A> tag.

WML also has hyperlinks. As you might expect from the other user interaction elements you've seen in this chapter, they aren't limited to simply going to another place. WML hyperlinks use tasks to allow them to control just about anything useful.

Hyperlinks are put into a page using the <anchor> element. It takes only one attribute:

title *(optional variable string)*

Provides an optional title to the element. As with the label attribute on the <do> element, you should try to keep this to six or fewer characters, and the browser is free to ignore it. This is rarely used in practice, as there is already the linked text inside the <anchor> to provide a label.

The <anchor> element must contain two things: a task element that is performed when the element is activated and some text or images to which to attach the link. A simple example of the <anchor> element is:

```
<anchor>next page<go href="page17.wml"/></anchor>
```

Figure 4-1. Menu of available pages

This attaches a link to the words next page, so that selecting them sends the browser to the URL *page17.wml.*

The most common tasks to use with <anchor> elements are <go> tasks. For other kinds of tasks, consider using <do> elements instead. For example, if you want a control to activate a <prev> task, you should strongly consider simply using a <do> with type set to prev. It's best to use <anchor> only where it's important that the control is kept with the text surrounding it.

The <a> Element

If you've done much work with HTML, the **<anchor>** element may seem like a lot of typing. Sure, it's more flexible than HTML's **<A>** tag, but it seems much nicer to simply type:

```
<A HREF="somewhere">linked text</A>
```

than it is to type:

```
<anchor><go href="somewhere"/>linked text</anchor>
```

Fear not: the designers of WML also recognized this fact and provided WML with the **<a>** element. (The name must be a lowercase **a**.) It's a useful shorthand for this simple case of the **<anchor>** element, which also has the benefit of looking familiar to HTML developers. It takes two attributes:

title *(optional variable string)*
> This has exactly the same effect as the **title** attribute on the **<anchor>** element. It provides an optional title for the element, which some browsers may use in displaying it. The same caveats apply: it's wise to keep the length to at most six characters, and the browser is free to ignore the attribute (as indeed most do).

href *(required variable URL)*
> Specifies the URL to go to when the link is activated.

For example, the element:

```
<a title="Next" href="page17.wml">Next Page</a>
```

is exactly equivalent to:

```
<anchor title="Next">
    <go href="page17.wml"/>
    Next Page
</anchor>
```

The form using the **<a>** element is also more efficient than the form using **<anchor>**, as there is less to transmit to the browser. Try to use the **<a>** form wherever possible.

The tabindex Attribute

Some browsers can cycle through **<input>** and **<select>** in a card using some sort of **TAB** key or similar control. Normally, the order in which this happens is chosen by the browser (usually the order in which the elements are specified in the card). The **tabindex** attribute allows this order to be changed for some or all of the elements in a card.

Not all browsers support this feature, as it doesn't fit into all of the user interfaces. If this feature is supported, the browser sorts all the <input> and <select> elements with a tabindex specified in ascending order. Pressing the TAB key (or whatever normally cycles through such elements) then selects these elements in this order. Any elements in the card without a tabindex specified are selected last.

Example 4-4 shows how this attribute can be used. The user is asked for a normal postal address. Both the county and nation fields have no tabindex: nation because it has a default, and county because it's usually unnecessary to give a county or state if the postal code is correct. The <do> element at the end calls a WMLScript function to check that the values are acceptable (for example, if no postal code is given, a county is required).

Example 4-4. Use of the tabindex Attribute

```
<?xml version="1.0"?>
<!DOCTYPE wml PUBLIC
    "-//WAPFORUM//DTD WML 1.1//EN"
    "http://www.wapforum.org/DTD/wml_1.1.xml">

<wml>
    <card title="Enter address">
        <p>Street:
            <input name="street" tabindex="1"/></p>
        <p>Town/City:
            <input name="town" tabindex="2"/></p>
        <p>County/State/Province:
            <input name="county"/></p>
        <p>Postal/Zip Code:
            <input name="code" tabindex="3"/></p>
        <p>Nation:
            <input name="nation" value="uk"/></p>
        <do type="accept" label="OK">
            <go href="address.wmlsc#check()"/>
        </do>
    </card>
</wml>
```

5

WML Timers

The previous chapters described how to interact with users in WML. Sometimes, however, you may want something to happen without the user explicitly having to activate a control.

To take a common example, suppose you want to display a company logo when the user connects to your WAP service. On a web page, you'd keep the image for the logo on screen the whole time, but WAP devices have limited screen sizes, and you can't afford to waste the space.

You could put the image at the top of the first page and let the user scroll down, but cell phone keypads are fiddly, and you'd prefer that the user didn't have to mess around to see the rest of the service. The same thing rules out a "click to enter" type of control.

What you really want is for the logo to be displayed for a second or two so that the user sees it, and for him to then be transported automatically to the main card. This can be done with a WML timer.

Using Timers with WML

A WML card may have a timer. Whenever the card is entered (whether forwards, as the result of a <go> task, or backwards, as the result of a <prev> task), the timer is initialized with a timeout value and started (unless the timeout is zero, in which case the timer never starts).

Once the timer has started, it counts down either until the count reaches zero or until a task is executed. If a task is executed, the timer is simply stopped beforehand. (Note, however, that a <noop> task doesn't affect the timer at all.) If the count reaches zero, however, an **ontimer** event is triggered on the card containing the timer. This event should be bound to a task, either with an `<onevent>` element or with the `ontimer` attribute of the `<card>` element.

A Simple Example

Before looking in depth at the elements that make timers work, Example 5-1 shows the simplest way to display a logo for a short time and then go to the main card. The image is displayed for one second, and then the second card is displayed. There is also a `<do>` element that allows the user to go directly to the second card without having to wait for the timer.

Example 5-1. Displaying a Logo

```
<?xml version="1.0"?>
<!DOCTYPE wml PUBLIC
    "-//WAPFORUM//DTD WML 1.1//EN"
    "http://www.wapforum.org/DTD/wml_1.1.xml">

<wml>
    <card title="Welcome" ontimer="#main">
        <!-- Timer waits 10 tenths of a second. -->
        <timer value="10"/>
        <p><img src="logo.wbmp"/></p>
        <do type="accept"><go href="#main"/></do>
    </card>

    <card title="Main" id="main">
        <p>Welcome to the main page!</p>
    </card>
</wml>
```

This particular effect is widespread in WML content at the time of writing. If you use it, make sure that the timeout is neither too short (some cell phones are very slow at downloading and rendering images, and the user may never see the logo), or too long (more than two seconds will irritate the user).

The ontimer Event

The `ontimer` event is triggered when a card's timer counts down from one to zero, which means that it doesn't occur if the timer is initialized to a timeout of zero.

You can bind a task to this event with the `<onevent>` element. For example, here's a way to return to the previous card when the timer expires:

```
<onevent type="ontimer">
    <prev/>
</onevent>
```

As with the `onenterforward` and `onenterbackward` events, there's a simple form of this event binding in the case where it's a simple `<go>` task (without `<setvar>` or `<postfield>` elements). For example, consider this binding:

```
<card title="simple go">
    <onevent type="ontimer">
        <go href="foo.wml"/>
    </onevent>

    <!-- rest of card, including timer itself -->
</card>
```

You can write it more compactly as:

```
<card title="simple go" ontimer="foo.wml">
    <!-- rest of card, including timer itself -->
</card>
```

The <timer> Element

A timer is declared inside a WML card with the `<timer>` element. It must follow the `<onevent>` elements if they are present. (If there are no `<onevent>` elements, the `<timer>` must be the first element inside the `<card>`.) No more than one `<timer>` may be present in a card.

The `<timer>` element takes two attributes:

name *(optional name)*

Name of a variable to use when initializing the timer. If this variable is set when the timer needs to be initialized, its value is used as the timeout. In addition, whenever the timer is stopped, the amount of time remaining is stored back into this variable. (If the timer expires, the value 0 is stored.)

value *(required variable number)*

Gives a default value for the timeout. This value is used if the **name** attribute isn't present or the variable that it names isn't set. If **name** is both present and names a variable containing a value, this attribute is ignored.

Timeouts are specified in units of a tenth of a second, but a particular browser may round them to some other precision internally. For example, a browser that can count only whole seconds can round all timeouts to the nearest second. If the initial timeout (from either the **name** variable or the **value** attribute) isn't a positive integer, the timer is ignored.

Because of these considerations, it's wise to always provide an alternative method of activating a timer's task. For example, add a <do> element with the same task to the card.

The <refresh> task has particular relevance to timers. Executing a <refresh> task stops the timer and stores the remaining time into the **name** variable if it's present, just as for any other task. However, when the <refresh> task completes, the browser is still in the same card, and so the timer is reinitialized and restarted.

This means that you can change the value of a timer's **name** variable in a <refresh> task, and the timer restarts with the new timeout. In this way, a <refresh> task that is triggered by a timer can restart the timer.

A Complicated Example

To take a much more complicated example, Example 5-2 shows how a <refresh> task can display three different images in sequence. The first one displays for half a second, and the other two display for one second each, after which the sequence repeats.

This is done by keeping the names of the images in the variables **img0**, **img1**, and **img2** and the timeouts in **time0**, **time1**, and **time2**. At all times, **img0** and **time0** refer to the currently displaying image; **img1** and **time1** refer to the next, and so on. The <refresh> task bound to the **ontimer** event contains six <setvar> elements, which cycle these variables around. (Read Chapter 2, *WML Variables and Contexts*, again if you don't remember how this works.)

Note that the timer doesn't simply reference the **time0** variable in its name attribute:

```
<timer name="time0"/>
```

This would set **time0** to zero when the timer expired, and the cycle wouldn't repeat. Instead, the <timer> element simply uses the current value of the **time0** variable:

```
<timer value="$(time0)"/>
```

The **onenterforward** event is also bound to a <refresh> task, which serves to initialize all the variables used by the cycling.

One of the problems with complicated examples like this is that some browsers don't support all the features required. (Fortunately, most uses of timers are much simpler; many almost identical to Example 5-1.)

For example, a number of browsers at the time of writing don't correctly restart timers after a `<refresh>` task, so they show the first image and change correctly to the second, but then stop.

In some other browsers, the `onenterforward` attribute stops the timer from ever being started, due to bugs within the browser.

What this all means is that you shouldn't rely on this sort of code working as it should. As the technology gets more mature and the browsers are debugged, things will improve, but never take it for granted!

Example 5-2. Displaying Three Images

```
<?xml version="1.0"?>
<!DOCTYPE wml PUBLIC
    "-//WAPFORUM//DTD WML 1.1//EN"
    "http://www.wapforum.org/DTD/wml_1.1.xml">

<wml>
    <card title="Three Images">
        <onevent type="onenterforward">
            <refresh>
                <setvar name="img0" value="first.wbmp"/>
                <setvar name="img1" value="second.wbmp"/>
                <setvar name="img2" value="third.wbmp"/>
                <setvar name="time0" value="5"/>
                <setvar name="time1" value="10"/>
                <setvar name="time2" value="10"/>
            </refresh>
        </onevent>
        <onevent type="ontimer">
            <refresh>
                <setvar name="img0" value="$(img1)"/>
                <setvar name="img1" value="$(img2)"/>
                <setvar name="img2" value="$(img0)"/>
                <setvar name="time0" value="$(time1)"/>
                <setvar name="time1" value="$(time2)"/>
                <setvar name="time2" value="$(time0)"/>
            </refresh>
        </onevent>

        <timer value="$(time0)"/>

        <p><img src="$(img0)" alt="[image]"/></p>
    </card>
</wml>
```

Finally, Example 5-3 shows how the **name** attribute works. The timer is started with a timeout of one minute. At any time, the user can activate the <do> element and go to the second card, which reports how much time is remaining on the timer. Returning to the first card restarts the timer where it left off. When the timer finally expires, the user is transported to the third card.

Example 5-3. Timer with name

```
<?xml version="1.0"?>
<!DOCTYPE wml PUBLIC
    "-//WAPFORUM//DTD WML 1.1//EN"
    "http://www.wapforum.org/DTD/wml_1.1.xml">

<wml>
    <card title="First card" id="one" ontimer="#three">
        <timer name="timeout" value="600"/>

        <p>The timer is running...</p>
        <do type="" label="Check"><go href="#two"/></do>
    </card>

    <card title="Second card" id="two">
        <p>Time remaining:
            $(timeout) tenths of a second</p>
        <do type="prev" label="Back"><prev/></do>
    </card>

    <card title="Third card" id="three">
        <p>Timer expired!</p>
    </card>
</wml>
```

6

WML Decks, Templates, and Cards

Now that you've seen some of the interesting things you can put into a deck, it's time to revisit those very first WML elements we saw back in Example 1-1. You can see them in more detail in the light of what you now know about WML; particularly events (Chapter 3, *WML Tasks and Events*) and the <do> element (Chapter 4, *WML User Interaction*).

The <wml> Element

The <wml> element serves a purpose much like the <HTML> element does for HTML pages: it encloses the entirety of the deck. Effectively, a WML deck consists of a single <wml> element. It doesn't take any attributes.

The <head> Element

The <head> element in WML is similar to the <HEAD> element in HTML: it marks a place for *meta-information* about the document to be stored. Meta-information is information about the document itself, rather than its content. If present, the <head> element must be the first thing inside the <wml> element. It doesn't take any attributes.

The <access> Element

The <access> element provides a simple form of *access control* for a deck. This allows a deck to specify that only certain other decks may link to it (these decks are known as *referring URLs*). Since this control is performed in the browser, not the server, there is no real security in this mechanism, and hence it's probably of limited use. There may be no more than one <access> element in a deck, and it must be the first thing inside the <head> element.

Attributes of the <access> Element

domain *(string; optional; default same as deck's domain)*

> Specifies the domain (effectively, the range of servers) from which the refer-ring deck must come. This must match against whole components (parts of the name between dots) at the end of the server name. If this attribute is omit-ted, its value defaults to the server from the new deck's URL.

> For example, if the attribute domain="wml.wap.net" is specified:

wml.wap.net
> Matches; access is permitted.

www.wml.wap.net
> Matches; access is permitted.

www.test.wml.wap.net
> Matches; access is permitted.

wapforum.org
> Doesn't match; access is denied.

wap.net
> Doesn't match the whole domain; access is denied.

otherwml.wap.net
> otherwml doesn't match wml (must match whole components); access is denied.

path *(string; optional; default /)*

> Specifies the path within the referring URL that must match. (The path is the part of the URL that specifies a file or directory on the server.) This must match against whole components (parts between slashes) at the beginning of the path of the referring URL. If it's omitted, it defaults to /: that is, any file on any server that matches the domain attribute. If it's specified without a lead-ing slash, it's taken relative to the path from the new deck's URL.

> For example, if the attribute path="/foo" is specified:

/foo/deck.wml
> Matches; access is permitted.

/foo/bar/deck.wml
> Matches; access is permitted.

/bar/deck.wml
> Doesn't match; access is denied.

/foobar/deck.wml

> `foobar` doesn't match `foo` (must match whole components); access is denied.

The *<meta>* Element

The `<meta>` element places an item of arbitrary meta-information in a WML deck. This item is structured as a *property name* and its *value*. You can put any number of `<meta>` elements into the `<head>` element. This can add keywords for indexing purposes, store hints about the content of the deck, and store any other information. No standard properties have yet been defined for WML, but conventions will develop, just as they did with HTML.

> Note that some browsers may not support all the features of the `<meta>` element.

Attributes of the *<meta>* Element

`name` *(string; optional)*

> Gives the name of this property. Meta-information with this attribute is intended for server-side applications, so it may be removed before it gets to the browser.

`http-equiv` *(string; optional)*

> An alternative for the `name` attribute (you can't specify both on the same `<meta>` element). If this attribute is present, it specifies that the property should be sent to the browser via HTTP or WSP headers (WAP gateways and WSP headers are explained in Appendix B, *WAP Gateways and WSP*). For example, this element tells any proxy servers or gateways (as well as the browser itself) not to cache the deck:
>
> ```
> <meta http-equiv="Cache-control" content="no-cache"/>
> ```

`forua` *(boolean; optional)*

> If present and set to `true`, indicates that the property is intended for the use of the browser. (ua comes from *user agent*, the term that the WAP specifications use to refer to the browser.)

`content` *(string; required)*

> Specifies the value of the property (remember that properties have a name and a value). This attribute must be provided; the `<meta>` element is meaningless without it.

scheme *(string; optional)*

> Can specify a format or structure that some properties may need to interpret their values. This attribute is used by few properties.

The <card> Element

As you saw back in Example 1-1, the <card> element encloses a WML card within a deck. In addition, text and graphics enclosed within <p> elements, it may also contain a number of event bindings (see Chapter 3) and a timer (see Chapter 5, *WML Timers*).

Attributes of the <card> Element

title *(variable string; optional)*

> Gives a title to this card. This title is displayed in some way by the browser when the card is visible.

newcontext *(boolean; optional; default* false*)*

> Specifies that when this card is entered, the browser context should be cleared: all variable bindings are removed, and the history stack is emptied. This happens before the **onenterforward** event binding is executed, so new variables may be set up there.

ordered *(boolean; optional; default* true*)*

> Provides a hint to the browser about how the card is organized. Set it to **true** if the card consists of a number of separate fields that should be dealt with in the order they appear in the card. Set it to **false** if the card contains optional fields or may be filled in out of order. At the time of writing, no WAP browsers support the **ordered** attribute.

onenterforward *(variable url; optional)*
onenterbackward *(variable url; optional)*
ontimer *(variable url; optional)*

> These three attributes exist as a shorthand for including simple <onevent> event bindings inside the <card> element. You can use these when the task to be performed is a simple <go> task. This task (because it's simplified to just the URL) can't set any variables or contain any postfields, and its method is limited to GET.

The <template> Element

The <template> element provides an interesting WML feature not found in HTML. When you write a deck containing several cards, you may find that parts of the structure are common to all the cards. For example, it's fairly typical for each card to have a "back" control and a "home" control. These controls are normally implemented as <do> elements. It would be convenient to specify these common elements once per deck rather than once per card, and that is just what the <template> element allows.

It doesn't stop there, though. Remember all those card events from Chapter 3? Wouldn't it be easier to set up bindings for all the events just once for the whole deck? That would certainly save wear and tear on your fingers (or at least your cut-and-paste keys), and since WAP is supposed to be optimized for low band-width, it's a waste of time to have to send all that duplicated information. As you might have guessed, the <template> element allows this, too.

You may be wondering what happens if you want a control on most, but not all, of the cards in a deck, or if you want an event binding to apply to just some of the cards. The good news is that this case has also been anticipated: any individual card can override the deck-level settings with its own, or even remove controls or event bindings altogether. This process of overriding is known as *shadowing* (see the next section for an explanation of shadowing).

The <template> element can contain any number of <do> elements to provide the various controls. It can also provide up to three <onevent> bindings, one to each of the **enterforward**, **enterbackward**, and **timer** events. If present, each applies to every card in the deck unless shadowed.

Shadowing

To *shadow* an event binding is to override it with another event binding. Shadow-ing an event binding in a particular card is simple: simply add a new binding for the event to the card in question, and this binding takes precedence over the deck-level binding from the <template>. To remove a binding altogether in a particular card, shadow it with an event binding that contains a <noop> task.

Shadowing a deck-level <do> control is slightly more involved, as there can be more than one. This is where the **name** attribute of the <do> comes in. Give the <do> you want to shadow some unique name in its **name** attribute, and then put this same name in the **name** attribute on the <do> that replaces it (the replace-ment must also have the same **type**). As with event bindings, if a deck-level <do> is shadowed with the <noop> task, it disappears altogether.

Attributes of the <template> Element

onenterforward *(variable url; optional)*
onenterbackward *(variable url; optional)*
ontimer *(variable url; optional)*

These three attributes behave just like their equivalents for the **<card>** element: they provide a shorthand for the commonest form of event bindings. The only difference is that here they set deck-level rather than card-level event bindings.

Examples of the <template> Element

Example 6-1 gives an example of a simple template. This adds a "back" control to each card in the deck and also a deck-level event binding so that the variable **secret** is cleared whenever any card in the deck is entered forwards.

Example 6-1. A Simple Template

```
<?xml version="1.0"?>
<!DOCTYPE wml PUBLIC
    "-//WAPFORUM//DTD WML 1.1//EN"
    "http://www.wapforum.org/DTD/wml_1.1.xml">

<wml>
    <template>
        <do type="prev" title="Back"><prev/></do>
        <onevent type="onenterforward">
            <refresh>
                <setvar name="secret" value=""/>
            </refresh>
        </onevent>
    </template>

    <card title="Card 1" id="card1">
        <p>This is card 1.</p>
        <p><a href="#card2">go to card 2</a></p>
    </card>

    <card title="Card 2" id="card2">
        <p>This is card 2.</p>
        <p><a href="#card3">go to card 3</a></p>
    </card>

    <card title="Card 3" id="card3">
        <p>This is card 3.</p>
        <p><a href="somewhere_else.wml">
            go somewhere else</a></p>
    </card>
</wml>
```

Example 6-2 extends Example 6-1 to show how both `<do>` elements and event
bindings at the deck level can be shadowed to override their effect for individual
cards. Here, the first card has no back button, and the third doesn't clear the
secret variable when entered.

Example 6-2. A Template with Shadowing

```
<?xml version="1.0"?>
<!DOCTYPE wml PUBLIC
    "-//WAPFORUM//DTD WML 1.1//EN"
    "http://www.wapforum.org/DTD/wml_1.1.xml">

<wml>
    <template>
        <do type="prev" title="Back" id="prev-ctrl">
            <prev/>
        </do>
        <onevent type="onenterforward">
            <refresh>
                <setvar name="secret" value=""/>
            </refresh>
        </onevent>
    </template>

    <card title="Card 1" id="card1">
        <do type="prev" id="prev-ctrl"><noop/></do>
        <p>This is card 1.</p>
        <p><a href="#card2">go to card 2</a></p>
    </card>

    <card title="Card 2" id="card2">
        <p>This is card 2.</p>
        <p><a href="#card3">go to card 3</a></p>
    </card>

    <card title="Card 3" id="card3">
        <onevent type="onenterforward"><noop/></onevent>
        <p>This is card 3.</p>
        <p><a href="somewhere_else.wml">
            go somewhere else</a></p>
    </card>
</wml>
```

7

WML Text and Text Formatting

By this point, you have seen how to create all sorts of interactive applications in WML and how to use variables, tasks, and events to do things that would require serious server-side processing in HTML.

Now that there aren't any exciting new features to cover, it's time to go back to simple text and see what can be done with it to make it more interesting. This is an area where WML is seriously lacking in comparison to HTML, which provides all sorts of features for changing the size, style, typeface, and color of text, as well as powerful support for tables.

One reason for not covering this topic earlier is that it shouldn't be your major concern when creating WML. Most cell phone browsers simply ignore all these text-formatting options, so a large number of users never see all the styles you spend so long choosing. Text style changes can be used to make your WAP content look much more attractive on PDAs and future smart cell phones, but you should not think of them as more than just little decorations to be added on once everything is working properly. Even features such as tables and centered or right-aligned text are not guaranteed to be present in all browsers. Having said that, the first element we look at is one that's always present in some form—the `<p>` element.

The `<p>` Element

As you saw back in Example 1-1, the `<p>` element marks a paragraph of text in a WML card. All body text, user controls (such as `<input>` and `<select>` elements), and images must appear within a `<p>` element. Most browsers ignore any that fall outside a `<p>`, but some actually reject the deck and refuse to display it. The one exception to this rule is the `<do>` element, which may appear either inside or outside a `<p>`. (It's actually regarded as better style to leave it outside the `<p>`.)

Normally, the <p> element is used without attributes, which results in the text in the paragraph being left-aligned and wrapped into lines to fit on the screen. It can also take two attributes to control how the text is presented, assuming of course that the browser is able (and willing) to display text with different alignments or to display nonwrapped text.

A paragraph with no content other than possibly some whitespace is referred to as *insignificant*. Such paragraphs are ignored by the browser: they can't add blank lines between paragraphs, and even their attributes are ignored. (Normally, the mode attribute applies to subsequent paragraphs until another mode is specified; this doesn't happen with insignificant paragraphs.) Some WAP gateways may even strip insignificant paragraphs out of the deck before sending it to the browser.

Attributes of the <p> Element

align *(optional string; default* left*)*
> Specifies the alignment for the text in this paragraph. The following are legal values for this attribute:

left
> Align to left margin: right side is ragged.

right
> Align to right margin: left side is ragged.

center
> Center the text onscreen.

> Note that there's no way to specify that the text be aligned on both left and right (known as *justified* text).

mode *(optional string; default same as previous paragraph)*
> Specifies whether or not the text in this paragraph should be wrapped. If set to wrap, the text is broken into lines to fit on the screen. If set to nowrap, this doesn't happen, and the user has to scroll the display sideways to see the end of long lines. Some browsers are known to ignore this attribute, probably because they don't want the trouble of handling horizontal scrolling. If mode isn't specified, the paragraph has the same mode as the last paragraph that specified one, or wrap if no previous paragraph has an explicit mode. This isn't the same as the behavior of align, which defaults to left if not specified.

The
 Element

The <br> element is one of the simplest in WML. It takes no attributes and is always specified as an empty-element tag, <br/>. It marks a line break in a paragraph of text: when the browser encounters a <br/>, it starts a new line.

You may ask what the difference is between using a **
** to break lines:

```
<p>text<br/>more text</p>
```

and using another paragraph:

```
<p>text</p><p>more text</p>
```

The answer is that WAP doesn't specify the difference. Some browsers insert a small amount of blank space between paragraphs, but won't do this at a **
, but not all browsers actually make a distinction at all. Note that if you need to change the alignment or wrapping mode of the text, you have to use a **<p>, since the **
** tag can't specify these attributes.

A good rule of thumb is to use **<p>** where the text naturally breaks into blocks, just like the paragraphs in normal text. Use **
** where you want a break for presentation, but the text continues with part of the same block afterward. For example, when putting normal paragraphs of text into a deck, use one **<p>** element for each paragraph:

```
<p>
    A good rule of thumb is to use &lt;p&gt; where the
    text naturally breaks into blocks, just like the
    paragraphs in normal text. Use &lt;br/&gt; where
    you want a break for presentation, but the text
    continues with part of the same block afterward.
</p>
<p>
    For example, when putting normal paragraphs of
    text into a deck, use one &lt;p&gt; element for
    each paragraph:
</p>
```

When entering something like a postal address, which is normally formatted into lines but still forms a single logical block, use one **<p>** for the block and a **
** between each line:

```
<p>
    O&apos;Reilly &amp; Associates, Inc.<br/>
    101 Morris Street<br/>
    Sebastopol<br/>
    CA 95472<br/>
    USA
</p>
```

Character Formatting

The support for character formatting in WML is quite limited compared to HTML. There is no support for specifying the color or typeface of the text, size changes are limited to "bigger" or "smaller," and there's no guarantee that any of these choices will be honored anyway.

Support is provided through seven elements. None take any attributes, and their effect applies to all the text they enclose. The browser is free to ignore any or all these attributes if it chooses or if its screen display can't cope with them.

Emphasis

These two elements provide some kind of emphasis. The exact form this takes isn't specified: some browsers may use style changes such as boldface or italics to emphasize the text, some may change the color, and some may ignore it altogether. These tags are the most likely of the character formats to be supported, and so you should use these in preference to the other formats. If you don't need a specific style but just want some text to stand out, you should use the following two tags instead of <b>, <i>, and <u>:

<em>
> Emphasis

<strong>
> Strong emphasis

Size Changes

These two elements provide simple size changes in the text:

<big>
> Larger font size

<small>
> Smaller font size

Style Changes

These three elements provide simple text-style changes. Because many browsers don't support these elements, you should use these only if you really need exact control over how the text is displayed:

<b> Boldface

<i> Italics

<u> Underlining

 Note that many browsers underline hyperlinks created with the <a> and <anchor> elements. To prevent visual confusion, you should probably avoid using the <u> formatting element.

Examples

These elements are simple to use. Normally, only a couple of words have a character format applied:

```
<p align="center"><big>
    Centered heading in larger text.
</big></p>

<p align="left">
Some text with bits in <b>bold</b> and <em>emphasis</em>.
</p>
```

The effect of combining multiple character formats is undefined. Some browsers may do their best to apply all of them, some may apply only one, and some may give up and use none. For example, you can specify boldface underlined text as:

```
<b><u>boldface underline</u></b>
```

There's no guarantee this will work, however. It may come out as just boldface, just underlined, or as neither. It's much safer to use the `<em>` and `<strong>` tags instead.

Tables

Tables are one of the worst-supported features in WML, at least in browsers available at the time of writing. The reason for this is that displaying tables properly (as laid down in the WAP specifications) often requires a lot of screen space, which is at a premium on devices such as cell phones. For example, at least one browser currently available displays each cell of a table on a new line, with lines of * characters to mark the places where rows should have started.

WML also doesn't allow user interface elements to appear in tables, except for anchored text (using the `<a>` or `<anchor>` elements). This makes it easier for those browsers that do support tables. You are, however, allowed images, text-style changes, and even line breaks.

WML tables include a number of rows, each containing a number of cells. The cells may themselves contain multiple lines of text, due to embedded `<br/>` tags, but these are all considered part of the same cell.

The <table> Element

This element declares a table in a WML card. It must appear inside a paragraph (in other words, inside a `<p>` element). A `<table>` contains nothing but `<tr>` elements giving its rows. It takes three attributes, giving details about the intended presentation of the table onscreen.

Attributes of the <table> element

columns *(required number)*

> Specifies the number of columns in the table. If a row (a <tr> element) has fewer than this number of cells (<td> elements), the browser pads it with empty cells at the end of the row. If it has more, the cells at the end of the row are merged, so that no extra columns are created.

title *(optional variable string)*

> Specifies an optional title for this table. The browser may use this to display the table.

align *(optional string)*

> Specifies the column alignments for this table. This is a list of characters, each giving the alignment for one column in order. The valid characters are:
>
> L   Cells are left-aligned within the column.
>
> R   Cells are right-aligned within the column.
>
> C   Cells are centered within the column.
>
> If there are fewer characters than columns (or if the attribute is omitted entirely), the remaining columns are left-aligned by default. For example, if the alignment string LLRC is specified for a seven-column table, it's equivalent to the string LLRCLLL, because the extra three columns are left-aligned by default. This in turn means that all columns are left-aligned, except for the third, which is right-aligned, and the fourth, which is centered.

The <tr> Element

Within a <table> element, the rows of the table are delimited by <tr> elements, each one representing a single row. These elements take no attributes and can contain only <td> elements, giving the cells within the row. It's legal for a <tr> element to contain no <td> elements or only empty ones. This indicates an empty row in the table.

The <td> Element

This element encloses a single cell within a table. It may appear only inside a <tr> element. It takes no attributes and may contain the following: flow text; images using the <img> element; text style changes using the <em>, <strong>, <b>, <i>, <u>, <big>, and <small> elements; and anchored text using the <a> or <anchor> elements.

An empty <td> element, or one containing only whitespace, is legal and significant. That cell is left empty when the table is displayed. If there are fewer <td> elements in a <tr> than the number of columns for the table, the last ones are assumed to be empty (as if they had each been specified as <td/>).

Example

Example 7-1 shows how a WAP shopping system can display the contents of the user's basket using a table. The three columns containing numbers or prices are right-aligned, the two columns that contain only @ or = signs are centered, and the item names are left-aligned. The line with the total contains empty cells to align the overall total with the column containing the row totals. In addition, the overall total is displayed in boldface with a <b> element, if the browser supports this feature.

Example 7-1. Shopping Basket with Tables

```
<?xml version="1.0"?>
<!DOCTYPE wml PUBLIC
    "-//WAPFORUM//DTD WML 1.1//EN"
    "http://www.wapforum.org/DTD/wml_1.1.xml">

<wml>
    <card title="Basket">
        <p align="center">
            <table columns="6" align="LRCRCR">
                <tr>
                    <td>floppy drive</td>
                    <td>1</td>
                    <td>@</td>
                    <td>$$29.95</td>
                    <td>=</td>
                    <td>$$29.95</td>
                </tr>
                <tr>
                    <td>floppy disk</td>
                    <td>10</td>
                    <td>@</td>
                    <td>$$0.75</td>
                    <td>=</td>
                    <td>$$7.50</td>
                </tr>
                <tr>
                    <td>TOTAL</td>
                    <td/><td/><td/>
                    <td>=</td>
                    <td><b>$$37.45</b></td>
                </tr>
            </table>
        </p>
    </card>
</wml>
```

Figure 7-1 shows a browser with good table support.

A browser with poor table support may render the same information in a format like Figure 7-2.

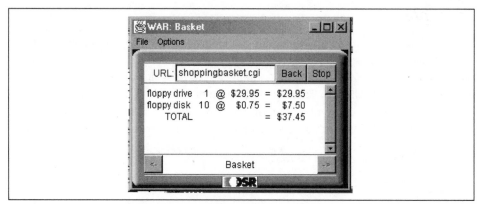

Figure 7-1. Shopping basket with good table support

Figure 7-2. Shopping basket with poor table support

8

WML Images

This chapter is the last one in this book dealing with WML, before we get into WMLScript. Therefore, it's finally time to get around to the subject of images in WML.

Why have I put this topic so late in the book? Because images should not be your major concern when writing WML. Most modern web pages rely heavily on images, so most books on HTML cover images quite early. When writing WML, however, you should remember that most WAP browsers are limited in terms of their image support.

In particular, screen sizes will often be quite small. One popular WAP cell phone at the time of writing has a total size of 96 by 64 pixels, and not all of that is available to display images. Most screens are black and white. Not even all PDAs have color screens, and cell phones with color are still very rare.

Not all browsers are capable of aligning images with other items: some simply ignore all the image alignment information and put each image on a line by itself. This means you shouldn't use images even for the bullets in a bulleted list because it would look silly if the images all appear on the line above the text they were supposed to be bulleting.

The <img> Element

Images are put into a WML page using the `<img>` element. If you're familiar with HTML, you'll recognize this tag, and it's indeed used in a similar way. Keep in mind that some browsers lay out images inline with text, while others place images on separate lines.

Attributes of the <img> Element

`src` *(required variable url)*

Specifies the URL from which to download the image.

`alt` *(required variable string)*

Specifies text to use instead of the image if it can't be displayed for some reason. For example, it's used if the image file can't be downloaded or if the browser doesn't support images at all.

`localsrc` *(optional variable string)*

Some browsers may provide images stored locally, rather than downloaded from the network. This attribute allows these images to be referenced from an `<img>` element. For example, a cell phone carrier could offer phones with images stored inside the phone and then reference these images in its own WAP service. Unless you are dealing with such a browser, you don't need to worry about this attribute. If you are dealing with such a browser, consult its documentation to find out the value you need to put into this attribute; the values differ from browser to browser.

`align` *(optional string; default* `bottom`*)*

Specifies how the image should be aligned vertically within the line of text. If set to `bottom` (the default), the bottom of the image is aligned with the baseline of the current line of text. (The *baseline* of a line of text is the line at the base of all the capital letters. The only parts of the text that go below the baseline are the "descenders" or tails of letters such as lowercase "p" and "g.") If set to `middle`, the center of the image is aligned with the center of the current line of text. If set to `top`, the top of the image is aligned with the top of the current line of text.

`hspace` *(optional length)*
`vspace` *(optional length)*

Specifies an amount of space (in pixels) to be inserted to the left and right (for **hspace**) or above and below (for **vspace**) the image as padding. If this is specified as a percentage, the value is taken as that percentage of the available space on the screen.

`width` *(optional length)*
`height` *(optional length)*

Specifies the size of the image, either in pixels or as a percentage of the screen size. If this is different from the actual size of the image when downloaded, the browser may choose to either ignore these values or scale the image to fit. (Most simply redraw the screen with the correct image size.) These values are simply a hint to the browser, to allow it to reserve space for images before it knows their sizes. The browser may ignore them.

Examples

To simply put an image on a line by itself, use:

```
<p><img src="image.wbmp" alt="[image]"/></p>
```

To use an image that adds the superscripted "TM" to indicate a trademark (assuming of course that the browser can actually align images properly), use:

```
Java<img src="tm.wbmp" alt="(TM)" align="top"/>
```

To center an image horizontally and vertically on the screen (if the browser supports this feature) use:

```
<p><img src="image.wbmp" alt="[image]" hspace="50%" vspace="50%"/></p>
```

The WBMP Image Format

You may have noticed that all the examples of the `<img>` element in this book have used image names ending with *.wbmp*. This is a special image format used in WAP. In fact, it's the only image format most browsers support. All WAP browsers that support images must support WBMP, so it's the safest choice if you want to include images in your WML.

WBMP stands for *wireless bitmap*, and it's a simple image format. Forget things like color, or animation, or even compression. (Image formats such as GIF and JPEG are the two most common on web pages; they compress the data to make the files smaller and faster to download.) WBMP files store only two things about the image: its size and a block of pixels, each of which is either black or white. There may be future versions with more features, but at the moment black and white is all there is.

To create the WBMP files, you need a converter. There are many of these available, some for free download.

One thing to bear in mind about small monochrome images such as these are that direct conversion from large, full-color images doesn't usually produce results that are anywhere near acceptable. Some company logos are simple images in only a few colors, and these can convert reasonably well, but images with subtle graduations of color convert very badly. The best solution is to use regular graphics touch-up software to convert the image to black and white and only then convert it to the WBMP format.

9

Introduction to WMLScript

Now that you have reached this point in the book, you should have a good idea of the things that can be done with WML alone: static page layouts and simple user interaction. Until now, the only way you could have any complicated interactions would be with some sort of dynamic content on the server.

Although WML provides variables, tasks, and events to make interaction much cleaner and easier, there are some tasks that can't be done in WML alone. If data must be checked for validity, for instance to make sure that a phone number really looks like a phone number or to check that a credit card number has the right number of digits, this checking has to be done by something outside WML.

The most obvious way to do this checking would be the way it was done on the Web for a long time: send the data to the server and let the server do the checking. This approach has one big problem, however: the time taken for the round trip to the server and back. Just think of the web sites where you enter your address, click OK, and wait the best part of a minute before they tell you that you haven't included a phone number.

A better approach is to do the checking on the browser, before sending anything to the server. This is exactly why WMLScript was designed.

WMLScript with WML

One of the most important things about WMLScript is how tightly it integrates with WML. You can put a call to WMLScript anywhere you can put a WML task. In the other direction, scripts can read and change browser variables and run tasks. (In fact, these are the only things a script can do.) These two things combine to make WMLScript extremely powerful. You can even write complete games using only WML and WMLScript.

WMLScript is called from WML using a `<go>` task with a specially formatted URL. This gives you great flexibility in where you put the calls to script functions: you can replace any task with a script call. (See Chapter 13, *WMLScript Functions*, for full details of how this is done.)

To demonstrate why WMLScript is such a benefit to WML, consider a form for entering a shipping address. There are fields for both the country and state. The state field must be filled in if the country is the United States; it's ignored otherwise. Because forgetting to enter the state is a common error, you should warn the user without him having to wait for the server to check the fields and send back a response, a process that can easily take several seconds. That is, the check should be done by the browser.

The WML fragment that produces these fields looks like this:

```
<p>State (US only): <input name="state" format="AA" emptyok="true"/></p>
<p>Country: <input name="country" format="AA" value="US"/></p>
```

Note the `format="AA"` attribute, which forces the field to be two uppercase letters.

This card also contains a WML `<do>` control, which sends the data to the server:

```
<do type="accept">
    <go href="address.cgi?s=$(state)&amp;c=$(country)"/>
</do>
```

The check is really very simple: if the country is "US," and the state field is empty, don't send the data to the server, but instead warn the user that he must enter a state.

Displaying the warning is easy. Simply add an extra card to the deck:

```
<card title="No State" id="nostate">
    <p>Since you live in the US, you must enter a state.
       Please go back and enter one.</p>
    <do type="prev"><prev/></do>
</card>
```

You can now display the warning by executing a `<go>` to the URL `#nostate`.

The problem is that WML doesn't provide a way to do even simple checks like this. There just isn't any way to check this without sending the data all the way to the server, having the server check the values and reject them, and then send an error message all the way back. Not without using WMLScript, that is.

WMLScript to the Rescue

To use WMLScript to solve this problem, the `<go>` task that sends the data to the server needs to be changed to call WMLScript instead of loading a WML card. (Don't worry about the details of this process. They are explained in later chapters.)

The new accept control looks like:

```
<do type="accept">
    <go href="check.wmls#check()"/>
</do>
```

The URL in the **<go>** task represents a call to a script function called **check**, which can be found in the script file **check.wmls**. The **check** function looks like this:

```
extern function check()
{
    var state = WMLBrowser.getVar ("state");
    var country = WMLBrowser.getVar ("country");

    /* If country is US, a state must be provided. */
    if (country == "US" && state == "") {
        WMLBrowser.go ("#nostate");
        return;
    }

    /* ... Check other possible mistakes in here ... */

    /* No errors found: send to server. */
    WMLBrowser.go ("address.cgi?s=" + state + "&c=" + country);
}
```

(Again, don't worry about the details for now.)

This means that with only a few lines of code you can save many needless round trips to the server and back. This generally improves the feel of your site from the user's point of view.

What Is WMLScript?

WMLScript is loosely based on JavaScript but is much simpler in order to reduce the requirements on the device running the browser. (JavaScript can require quite large amounts of memory, and the interpreter to run it is complex.)

If you've ever done any programming in Java, JavaScript, C, C++, ECMAScript, or any of the large variety of other languages that borrow bits of syntax from each other, then a lot of the syntax of WMLScript should look familiar.

For example, a WMLScript function to calculate the factorial of a positive integer can be written as:

```
/* Calculate factorial of n. */
function factorial (n)
{
    var result = 1;

    for (var i=2; i<n; i++) {
```

```
        result *= n;
    }

    return result;
}
```

The curly braces, the `for` statement in the middle, and the `return` statement at the end are all similar to languages such as C, Java, JavaScript, or C++. The `function` line and the `var` line may be less familiar; they will be covered in later chapters.

WMLScript comments can have two forms: like in C, starting with `/*` and continuing until `*/` even across lines, and like in C++, starting with `//` and continuing until the end of the line:

```
/* C comments look like this. */

// C++ comments look like this.

/*
    C comments may span
    as many lines as you like.
*/

// C++ comments must have a
// new // at the start of every
// line of the comment.
```

Everything in WMLScript is case-sensitive, including function names, variable names, literal values, keywords, and everything else.

Spacing, however, is flexible. Anywhere you can put a space, you can put as many as you want and also include such items as linebreaks and tabs, which are all counted simply as spaces. In addition, the only spaces that are actually required are those necessary to stop one symbol from being recognized as another or those between keywords. For example, in the code snippet:

```
if (x)
    a = b;
else if (y)
    foo (c, d);
```

the only space that is actually required is the one between `else` and `if`, because it separates two keywords. The fragment can also be written:

```
if(x)a=b;else if(y)foo(c,d);
```

without changing its behavior at all. The only reason for all the extra spaces in the first version is readability.

Standard Libraries

Because the WMLScript language itself has been simplified to the bare minimum, many common tasks can't be done directly. For example, there is no operator that can extract individual characters from strings. Fortunately, these missing functions are included in *standard libraries*, which are defined along with the WMLScript language and must be provided by all implementations. Therefore, they are effectively part of the language itself.

The libraries cover a wide range of functions, including conversions between different datatypes, string handling, and floating-point arithmetic. There are also high-level functions for dealing with URLs and displaying dialog boxes to the user. In addition, the interface with WML (the ability to manipulate browser variables and run tasks) is handled through the standard libraries.

Bytecode

To further ease the load on the device running the browser, WMLScript is compiled into a *bytecode* form before being transmitted.* This bytecode is effectively a series of instructions for a very simple computer, which makes the job of the WMLScript interpreter inside the device much easier. Because of this, the two terms *WMLScript interpreter* and *WMLScript virtual machine* (or *WMLScript VM*) are often used interchangeably.

It doesn't really need to concern you, though. The *WAP gateway* (covered in Appendix B, *WAP Gateways and WSP*) compiles your code for you if necessary. The only reason for doing it yourself is that you may have a compiler that does a better job, producing smaller or faster code, or you may want to hide your original source code from prying eyes. Either way, there's no difference in terms of the code you write, so just forget all about compilers and bytecode for now and concentrate on writing the code.

Functions

Like any good programming language, WMLScript supports functions, like the check() example given earlier in the chapter. In fact, WMLScript code is allowed only inside a function. This is similar to languages such as C and Java and different from languages such as JavaScript and Perl.

---

* WML is also converted into an internal binary form before being transmitted.

10

WMLScript Datatypes,
Variables, and Conversions

WMLScript is a weakly typed language. This means you never specify the datatype of a variable or the return type of a function. All expressions have a type internally, but WMLScript itself converts values back and forth between the different types as required, so that you don't have to.

For example, the value `1234` is an integer, but if you pass it to the `String. length()` library function, which expects a string, it's implicitly converted to the string `"1234"`, the length of which is 4.

Similarly, if you try to evaluate the expression:

```
"1234" * "2"
```

both values are converted to integers before use, and the result is the integer `2468`. This is what is meant by *weak typing*.

Datatypes and Literals

WMLScript has five datatypes: string, integer, floating-point number, Boolean, and the special type `invalid`. Every value in WMLScript belongs to one of these types, although most can be converted to others. The format of a literal value determines its type. (A *literal* is a constant included explicitly in the code.)

Strings

Strings in WMLScript can be any sequence of Unicode characters. They may be enclosed within either single or double quotes. The type of quotes used makes no difference to the string itself.

WMLScript supports special *escape sequences* to include special characters in strings. This can be used for nonprinting characters (such as newlines), characters that have a special meaning in strings (such as quotes), and characters that can't be entered in the source file (such as Chinese characters if your source file is in ASCII).*

WMLScript provides three ways to specify a specific Unicode character by number:

***nnn*

Represents the Unicode character given by the three octal digits *nnn*. This allows you to specify any of the low 256 Unicode characters, since the first octal digit may only be 0, 1, 2, or 3. These 256 characters include the whole of ASCII, so you can include any ASCII character using this form.

\\x*hh*

Represents the Unicode character given by the two hexadecimal digits *hh*. Just like the octal form, you can specify any of the low 256 Unicode characters like this.

\\u*hhhh*

Represents the Unicode character given by the four hexadecimal digits *hhhh*. This allows any Unicode character to be specified.

Table 10-1 shows special escape sequences, which represent specific characters.

Table 10-1. Special Escape Sequences

Escape Sequence	Character Represented	Unicode Equivalent
\'	Single quote	\u0027
\"	Double quote	\u0022
\\	Backslash	\u005C
\/	Forward slash	\u002F
\b	Backspace	\u0008
\f	Form feed	\u000C
\n	Newline	\u000A
\r	Carriage return	\u000D
\t	Horizontal tab	\u0009

Examples of valid string literals include:

```
""
'foo'
"Hello, World!"
'String with embedded single \' and double " quotes'
```

---

* The fact you can include Chinese characters doesn't mean the device can display them, however.

```
"String with embedded single ' and double \" quotes"
'Price is \24317 (seventeen pounds)'
"Price is $17 (seventeen dollars)"
'To include a backslash, use \\'
```

In WMLScript, the $ symbol isn't treated as a special character as it is in WML. As a result, you can put dollar signs into your strings, and they won't substitute any variables or do anything special. Similarly, the characters < and & aren't special in WMLScript, as they are in WML.

Integers

Integer values are stored as 32-bit signed integers. Literal integers may be specified in octal, decimal, or hexadecimal, but this does not affect the number itself: integers always display as decimal when converted to strings. The letters in hexadecimal literals may be in either upper- or lowercase.

Octal numbers start with the digit 0. Decimal numbers start with any nonzero digit. Hexadecimal numbers start with the sequence 0x. Examples of valid integer literals include:

```
17
42
0
0105
00007777
01232
0x00
0x2A
0x3e8
0x7fffffff
```

Floating-Point Numbers

Floating-point values in WMLScript are stored in IEEE single-precision format, which is a 32-bit floating-point format. This allows numbers up to approximately 3.4e+38 to be stored.

Not all WMLScript interpreters support floating-point numbers. The `Lang.float()` library function described in Chapter 15, *The Lang Library*, can find out if a given interpreter provides this support.

Floating-point literals can contain a decimal point and an exponent part (representing multiplication by a power of ten). This exponent is introduced by a letter e or E. Examples of valid floating-point literals include:

```
.0
0.0
0E+0
0e23
```

```
0.44
1.0
10E6
10e-6
123.456e-7
.42e+23
```

Note that the first four values all represent the same value, zero.

Booleans

WMLScript provides Boolean values, representing either true or false.

The two valid Boolean literals are:

```
true
false
```

Note that these literals are case-sensitive.

Invalid

The fifth WMLScript datatype, `invalid`, is an unusual one you probably haven't seen before. Its purpose is simply to represent a value that isn't any of the other types. This is often an error condition.

For example, the expression (1/2) gives a floating point value 0.5. The expression (1/0) can't be evaluated (division by zero is illegal), and so the result is `invalid`. Similarly, the library function for computing the square root of a number returns `invalid` when given a negative argument.

If required, you can also reference an `invalid` value literally, as:

```
invalid
```

Note that, although there is only one way to specify an `invalid` literal, all these values are treated as distinct. This means:

```
invalid == invalid
```

is never true, even though this may seem a little strange or even wrong.

In fact, the previous expression's result is also `invalid`. Almost all of the operators in WMLScript give an `invalid` result if *any* of their arguments are `invalid`. For example, all the following expressions evaluate to `invalid`:

```
1 + (1/0)
(1/0) == (-1/0)
1/(1/0)
```

The few exceptions to this rule will be pointed out as we encounter them later in the book.

Variables

WMLScript provides only local variables and access to the WML variables (which are always string-valued) from the browser context. There are no global variables, and there is no way to have any values persist from call to call. When a function returns, all its variables are lost.

A WMLScript variable can take a value of any of the five datatypes, including `invalid`. Variables are declared with the **var** statement. Any number of variables may be specified, separated by commas such as:

```
var foo;
var x, y, z;
var a, b, c, d, e, f, g, h, i, j;
```

Variables must be declared before use, so for example the following is incorrect:

```
function foo ()
{
    wibble = 2;
    var wibble;
}
```

All variables are implicitly initialized to the empty string, `""`. If some other initial value is required, an optional initializer may be included with the declaration:

```
var foo = 17, bar = 42;
```

This is completely equivalent to:

```
var foo, bar;
foo = 17;
bar = 42;
```

This means that the usual pattern of a WMLScript function is to first read variables out of the WML browser context, then process those values in some way, then write back new values to the context, and run a task (usually either a **<refresh>** or a **<go>**). For an illustration, see Example 10-1. The updated display reflects the new values of variables. I will return to browser variables in later chapters.

Example 10-1. Outline of a Function Called from WML

```
extern function called_from_wml ()
{
    /* First read variables from browser context.
     * These could also be passed in as function arguments.
     */
    var username = WMLBrowser.getVar ("username");
    var password = WMLBrowser.getVar ("password");

    /* Next, process those variables. */
    username = validate_username (username);
    password = validate_password (password);
```

Example 10-1. Outline of a Function Called from WML (continued)

```
    /* Write back new values. */
    WMLBrowser.setVar ("username", username);
    WMLBrowser.setVar ("password", password);

    /* Finally, a refresh task. */
    WMLBrowser.refresh ();
}
```

Variable Scope

Once declared, a variable remains in scope (that is, accessible) until the end of the function. The declaration takes place even if it occurs within an inner block, and even if the inner block is never executed (due to conditional processing). This sounds complicated but is really quite simple. For example:

```
function foo (x)
{
    if (x) {
        var y = 42;
    }

    return y;
}
```

The variable y is in scope from its declaration all the way to the end of the function, so the **return** statement is valid. This declaration takes place even if the condition x is false, so that the statement **var y = 42;** is never executed. However, the initialization of y to the value 42 takes place only if the **var** statement is actually executed. Thus, this function behaves as though it were written like this:

```
function foo (x)
{
    var y;

    if (x) {
        y = 42;
    }

    return y;
}
```

If this behavior seems confusing, simply declare all your variables at the top of the function, as in the final example. Then you can forget about the scoping rules.

Variable Names

Legal variable names in WMLScript contain only letters, digits, and underscores. The first character can't be a digit; it must be a letter or underscore.

A number of otherwise valid variable names are reserved by the WMLScript language itself and may not be used to name variables. For example, keywords such as for, function, and var are all illegal as variable names. The following words are all keywords:

access	agent	break	continue
div	domain	else	equiv
extern	for	function	header
http	if	isvalid	meta
name	path	return	typeof
url	use	user	var
while			

In addition, a number of words are also reserved for possible future extensions to the WMLScript language:

case	catch	class	const
debugger	default	delete	do
enum	export	extends	finally
import	in	lib	new
null	private	public	sizeof
struct	super	switch	this
throw	try	void	with

The following are all examples of legal variable names:

```
x
foo
___name_with_underscores___
ThisVariableNameIsImpracticalBecauseItIsTooLong
xy17
_0
```

The following are examples of illegal variable names:

```
17xy             (starts with a digit)
name with spaces (space isn't a letter, digit, or underscore)
while            (is a keyword)
switch           (is a reserved word)
```

Namespaces

WMLScript defines separate namespaces for function names, variable names, and URL pragmas (more on this last one later). This means you can have both a function called foo and a variable called foo, for example.

Type Conversion

WMLScript operators implicitly convert their operands into the types they require. For example, the * operator for multiplication can operate on either integers or floating points, so the operands must first be converted into one of these types.

If an argument can't be converted, the result is invalid. Note that there are no explicit conversions to invalid, since no operator actually requires an invalid value.

Conversion to String

* Integers convert to a string representing their value in decimal. For example, the integer 1234 converts to the string "1234", and the integer −42 converts to the string "-42".

* Floating-point numbers convert to a string representing their value. The exact form of this string may differ from implementation to implementation. For example, the floating-point number 0.2 may convert to any of the strings "0.2", "2e-1", ".2", "0.2e+0", and so on.

* Boolean true is converted to the string "true", and Boolean false is converted to the string "false".

* invalid can't be converted to a string.

Conversion to Integer

* A string containing a valid decimal integer is converted into that integer. Any other string can't be converted to an integer. For example, the strings "1234" and "+1234" both convert to the integer 1234, but the string "1234x" can't be converted.

* No floating-point value can be converted to an integer.

* Boolean true is converted to 1, and Boolean false is converted to 0.

* invalid can't be converted to an integer.

Conversion to Floating-Point Number

* A string containing a valid representation of a floating-point number is converted to that number. No other strings can be converted. For example, the string "5.0e-1" converts to the floating-point number 0.5; the string "5.0x" can't be converted.

If the conversion results in a number too big to represent in the single-precision floating-point format used, the conversion fails (and so the result is `invalid`).

If the conversion results in a floating-point underflow (a number very close to, but not actually zero), the result is taken as `0.0`. For example, the string `"1e999"` can't be converted, and the string `"1e-999"` converts to `0.0`.

- Integers are converted to the corresponding floating-point value.

- Boolean `true` is converted to floating-point `1.0`, and Boolean `false` is converted to floating-point `0.0`.

- `invalid` can't be converted to a floating-point number.

Conversion to Boolean

- The empty string is converted to `false`. All other strings are converted to `true`. This means `""` converts to `false`, but `"false"` converts to `true`!

- Integer 0 is converted to `false`. All other integers are converted to `true`. This behavior is similar to how the C language handles Boolean values.

- Floating-point `0.0` is converted to `false`. All other floating-point values are converted to `true`. This is similar to the conversion from integers to Booleans just mentioned.

- `invalid` can't be converted to a Boolean value.

11

WMLScript Operators and Expressions

Now that you know about WMLScript's datatypes, it's time to see how they can be linked with operators to form expressions.

If you know such languages as C or Java, the operators in this section will be familiar to you. Some of them have subtle differences, however, which are usually linked to WMLScript's dynamic typing. These differences will be pointed out as we encounter them.

Appendix C, *Summary of WMLScript Operators*, lists all the operators and summarizes their behaviors. If you know C or Java syntax, you may want to skip this chapter and check back only for the operators you're not familiar with. It's probably worth reading the next section, however, since this explains how the datatype conversion rules from Chapter 10, *WMLScript Datatypes, Variables, and Conversions*, apply to operators.

Operand Conversions

Some operators can take values of more than one type. For example, the * operator for multiplication can operate on either integers or floating-point numbers. WMLScript also defines which conversions are done in these cases:

- Operators that always take the same type of operands simply convert the arguments to those types. If the conversion fails, the result of the operation is invalid.

- Operators that take operands of any type simply use the values as they are. No conversion is performed because none is needed.

As you see from these rules, there can be unexpected gotchas: sometimes things don't do what you expect.

If you're not sure of the type of a value at a particular time, it's worth using standard library functions to explicitly force values to be converted. These functions will be described in Chapter 15, *The Lang Library*.

Unary Integer or Floating Point

Unary (one-argument) operators that take integers or floating-point numbers (such as unary + and −) first try to convert the operand to an integer. If this succeeds, the operation is performed on this integer, and the result is an integer.

If the conversion to integer fails, the operator tries to convert the operand to a floating-point number. If this succeeds, the operation is performed on this number.

If both attempts to convert (to both integer and floating point) fail, the result of the operation is `invalid`.

For example:

    +2 gives integer 2
    +2.0 gives floating-point 2.0
    -true gives integer -1
    -false gives integer 0
    +"123.456" gives floating-point 123.456
    +"a" gives invalid (can't be converted to integer or floating point)
    -"1e99" gives invalid (floating point out of legal range)

Binary Integer or Floating Point

Binary (two-argument) operators that take integers, or floating-point numbers (such as * and −), first try to convert both operands to integers. If this succeeds, the operation is performed on integers, and the result is an integer.

If either of the operands can't be converted to an integer, the operator tries to convert both to floating-point values. If this succeeds, the operation is performed on floating-point values, and the result is also a floating-point number.

If both conversion attempts fail, the result of the operation is `invalid`.

For example:

    3*4 gives integer 12
    3.0*4 gives floating-point 12.0

> "3"*4 gives integer 12
> "2"-"9" gives integer −7
> "2"-"9e0" gives floating-point −7
> 6.3*"x" gives invalid (can't be converted to integer or floating point)
> 0.1*"1e999" gives invalid (floating-point value out of range)

Integer, Floating Point, or String

Only one operator falls into this category: binary +, which is used not only for numbers, but also for string concatenation. For example, "x"+"y" evaluates to "xy".

If either operand is a string, this operator tries to convert the other to a string as well. If this succeeds, the two strings are concatenated and returned. If the second value can't be converted to a string, the result of the operation is invalid.

If neither operand is a string, the operator tries instead to convert both operands to integers. If this works, the two integers are added together, and the result is also an integer.

If the operands can't both be converted to integer, the + operator tries to convert them both to floating point. If that works, the two floating-point numbers are added together, and the result is a floating-point number.

If that conversion also fails, the result is invalid.

For example:

> "x"+"y" gives string "xy"
> "x"+1 gives string "x1"
> 1+"2" gives string "12"
> 1+2 gives integer 3
> 1+2e0 gives floating-point 3.0

Comparison Operators

The comparison operators (equals, less than, and so on) can also take operands as either strings, integers, or floating-point numbers. The difference from the + operator is that the result of the comparison is always a Boolean (unless all the attempts at conversion fail, in which case it's invalid).

If either operand is a string, the operator first attempts to convert the other into a string as well. If this succeeds, the two strings are compared in dictionary order.

If neither operand is a string, the operator attempts to convert both into integers. If this works, the two integers are compared.

The + Operator

The special handling of strings for the + operator can cause a variety of bugs. For example, take the case of 1+"2" giving string "12", rather than integer 3. Since 1-"2" and 1*"2" both behave as expected (giving the integer values -1 and 2, respectively), this is a case you need to watch for.

Another case to watch for is when you are reading numbers from browser variables (using standard library functions). Browser variables are always returned as strings, so the + operator may not do what you want. For example:

```
var count = WMLBrowser.getVar ("count");
count = count + 1;
```

This concatenates the character 1 to the end of the string, rather than adding 1 to the value. To add 1, you must write either:

```
var count = Lang.parseInt (WMLBrowser.getVar ("count"));
count = count + 1;
```

or:

```
var count = WMLBrowser.getVar ("count") - 0;
count = count + 1;
```

(This second example relies on the fact that subtracting zero from a value forces it to be converted to an integer or floating-point number.)

Hopefully, a future version of the WMLScript specification will correct this ambiguity and remove the need for these workarounds.

If the operands can't both be converted to integers, the operator tries to convert them to floating point, and if this works they are compared as floating point.

If all the conversions fail, the result of the comparison is invalid.

For example:

"FOO"<"foo" gives true (compared as strings)
2<"10" gives false (compared as strings: "2"<"10")
2<10 gives true (compared as integers)
1<"1e-6" gives true (compared as strings)
1<1e-6 gives false (compared as floating point: 1.0<0.000001)

Just as with the + operator, you need to watch very carefully if strings may be involved in the comparison. The case that 2>"10" (because character 2 compares greater than character 1) is especially worth bearing in mind!

Assignment Operators

Having expressions isn't much use unless you can assign them to variables, and assigning to variables is the purpose of the assignment operators. The left side of any assignment operator must be the variable to assign.

The most common assignment operator is the simplest, which simply assigns an expression to a variable. It's represented by =.

WMLScript also provides assignment operators that combine some other operator with the assignment. For example:

    x += y

is a short form of:

    x = (x + y)

There are 12 operators, each combining one of the simple binary operators with assignment: +=, -=, *=, /=, div=, %=, &=, |=, ^=, <<=, >>=, and >>>=. All the normal rules for each operator apply; so, for example, += can do string concatenation as well as addition, and /= always gives a floating-point result. Note that there are no assignment operators for the Boolean or comparison operators: if you really need that behavior, you have to write it out in full. (You probably won't need it, though.)

The result of any assignment operation is the value that was assigned. For example:

    foo (a = b)

sets **a** to the contents of **b** and then calls foo() with the new value of **a**. In the same way:

    foo (a *= b)

multiplies **a** by the contents of **b**, then calls foo() with the new value of **a**.

Arithmetic Operators

WMLScript provides all the normal arithmetic operators. The syntax for these is exactly the same as in C or Java.

The simplest two arithmetic operators are unary plus, represented by +, and unary minus, represented by -. Unary plus simply converts the value to a number,[*] and unary minus converts the value to a number, then negates it (subtracts it from zero).

---

[*] If it's already a number, no conversion is required. The phrase "convert to a number" really means "convert to a number if it isn't one already."

For example:

    +2 is integer 2
    -2 is integer -2
    -"-2" is integer 2
    -"2e0" is integer -2.0

After the unary operators, there are six binary arithmetic operators. Addition is represented by +, subtraction by -, and multiplication by *. There are two division operators: /, which operates on floating-point numbers and gives a floating-point result, and div, which operates on integers and gives an integer result. The final operator is the *modulo* or remainder operator, which gives the remainder after integer division and is represented by %.

All of these, other than div, should be familiar to you if you know C or Java. (C and Java use the datatypes of the operands and the result to determine whether to perform integer or floating-point division, so there's no need for the div operator.)

There's one slight complication to these operators: as mentioned in the "Operand Conversions" section earlier in this chapter, the + operator performs string concatenation rather than addition if either of its operands is a string. This can introduce subtle problems.

Examples:

    3 * 2 gives integer 6
    "3" * 2 gives integer 6
    3 / 2 gives floating-point 1.5
    3 div 2 gives integer 1
    3.0 div 2 gives invalid (3.0 can't be converted to integer)
    1 + 2 gives integer 3
    1 + 2.0 gives floating-point 3
    1 + "2" gives string "12"
    8 % 3 gives integer 2
    -8 % 3 gives integer -1
    8 % -3 gives integer 1
    -8 % -3 gives integer -2

Bitwise Operators

In addition to the normal arithmetic operators, WMLScript provides four operators for performing Boolean arithmetic on the bits that make up integers. These operators all operate only on integers, so if any operand can't be converted to an integer, the result of the operation is invalid.

Bitwise *complement* (also called bitwise *not*) flips every bit in its argument. (Every 0 bit becomes 1, and every 1 bit becomes 0.) It's represented by the ~ operator.

Bitwise *and, or,* and *exclusive or* each operate on two integers. For each bit position (32 of them), the bit in the result is set depending on the corresponding bits in the two operands. Bitwise *and* (represented by &) sets this bit if both operand bits are set, bitwise *or* (represented by |) sets it if either of the operand bits are set, and bitwise *exclusive or* (represented by ^) sets it if exactly one of the operand bits are set. This may sound complicated, but study the examples and it should become clear.

These operators all behave in exactly the same way as their counterparts in C and Java, so if you know either of those languages, you'll feel right at home.

Examples include (some numbers are in hexadecimal to make the bit patterns clearer):

```
0x0110 & 0x0011 gives integer 0x0010
0x0110 | 0x0011 gives integer 0x0111
0x0110 ^ 0x0011 gives integer 0x0101
6 & 3 gives integer 2
6 | 3 gives integer 7
6 ^ 3 gives integer 5
~1 gives integer 0xFFFFFFFE
~0 gives integer 0xFFFFFFFF
```

The bitwise operators aren't used often, so don't worry if they still seem confusing.

Shift Operators

As well as these operators to change individual bits, WMLScript also provides shift operators, which allow you to move all the bits in an integer left or right. Because of the way integers are represented, these can be used to multiply or divide integers by a power of two.

Shift right has two operators, >> and >>>. The difference between these two is that >> handles negative numbers properly, so you can always use it to do division by powers of two. On the other hand, >>> treats all numbers as unsigned, even though all integers in WMLScript are signed, and because of this it doesn't work as you'd expect for negative numbers. It's most often used, like the &, |, and ^ operators, when you use an integer just to store 32 separate bits, rather than a standard integer.

Shift left is represented by the << operator. It works for all numbers without requiring two operators.

All these shift operators require both their operands to be integers. In addition, the right operand (the number of places to shift) can't be negative. (This last condition isn't specified explicitly by the WMLScript specification, but different interpreters handle negative shift counts inconsistently.)

For example:

    10 << 3 gives 80 (equivalent to 10 * 2 * 2 * 2)
    10 >> 3 gives 1 (equivalent to 10 div 2 div 2 div 2)
    10 >>> 3 gives 1 (>> and >>> work the same for positive numbers)
    -10 << 3 gives -80 (equivalent to -10 * 2 * 2 * 2)
    -10 >> 3 gives -1 (equivalent to -10 div 2 div 2 div 2)
    -10 >>> 3 gives 536870911 (>>> doesn't handle negative numbers)

Although >> behaves almost exactly like integer division by a power of two, the result is rounded differently. The div operator always rounds toward zero, so for example:

    -1 div 2

gives zero. The >> operator, however, rounds negative numbers towards -1 rather than 0. (Positive numbers are always rounded towards zero.) This means that:

    -1 >> 1

gives -1, rather than 0 as div would.

This may all seem far more complicated than it should be: you may be wondering why you should bother with shifts, rather than just using * and div. The good news is that there is no real reason to use them if you don't want to. They are really just included for completeness and aren't used often in real WMLScript programs.

Logical Operators

The bitwise operators are all useful in their place, but far more often you just want a simple Boolean *and* or *or* operator that converts its operands to Boolean values rather than integers.

These operators (called *logical* operators to distinguish them from the bitwise operators) also perform *short-circuit evaluation*. This means that they evaluate their left operand first, and if that is enough to tell the final result, the right operand isn't evaluated.

Logical *and* is represented by &&. It evaluates its left operand first: if this converts to Boolean false, the result of the operation is false. If the left operand can't be converted to a Boolean, the result of the operation is invalid. In both cases, the right operand isn't evaluated at all. If, however, the left operand converts to Boolean `true`, the result of the operation is the right operand, converted to a Boolean value.

Logical *or* is represented by ||. It evaluates its left operand first. If this converts to Boolean `true`, the result of the operation is also `true`. Just like logical *and*, if the left operand can't be converted, the result of the operation is `invalid`. Also like the logical *and* operation, in both cases the right operand isn't evaluated at all. If the left operand converts to Boolean `false`, however, the result of the operation is the right operand, also converted to a Boolean value.

For example:

```
(1+1 == 2) || foo() gives true, with no call to foo()
(1+1 == 3) || foo() gives the result of foo() converted to Boolean
(1/0) || foo() gives invalid, with no call to foo()
(1+1 == 2) && foo() gives the result of foo() converted to Boolean
(1+1 == 3) && foo() gives false, with no call to foo()
(1/0) && foo() gives invalid, with no call to foo()
```

Increment and Decrement Operators

WMLScript provides four operators as a conveniently short form for the common task of adding or subtracting one from a variable.

The *preincrement* and *predecrement* operators, written as:

```
++var
```

and:

```
--var
```

respectively, each attempt to convert the contents of the variable to an integer or floating-point value, add one to it (++) or subtract one from it (--), and store it back into the variable. The result of the operator is the *new* value of the variable.

The *postincrement* and *postdecrement* operators, written as:

```
var++
```

and:

```
var--
```

respectively, behave slightly differently. They still change the value of the variable, but the result of the operator is the value of the variable before the change.

For example, suppose that variable a contains the value integer 42, b contains integer 0x7FFFFFFF (the largest valid positive integer value), c contains floating-point 2.3, d contains string "1e2", and e contains string "foo":

a++ gives integer 42 and sets a to integer 43

++a gives integer 43 and sets a to integer 43

a-- gives integer 42 and sets a to integer 41

--a gives integer 41 and sets a to integer 41

b++ gives integer 0x7FFFFFFF and sets b to invalid (overflow)

++b gives invalid and sets b to invalid (overflow again)

c++ gives floating-point 2.3 and sets c to floating-point 3.3

--c gives floating-point 1.3 and sets c to floating-point 1.3

d-- gives string "1e2" and sets d to floating-point 99.0

++d gives floating-point 101.0 and sets d to floating-point 101.0

e++ gives string "foo" and sets e to invalid (can't convert)

--e gives invalid and sets e to invalid (can't convert)

Note from these examples that the result of the postincrement and postdecrement forms is the value before the change is applied.

Another thing to note: even though these operators are valid to use in expressions, they are most often used alone, just for the side-effect of adding or subtracting one. For example, the increment operators are often used in a for loop:

```
for (var i=0; i<end; i++) {
    ...
}
```

This can also be written using preincrement:

```
for (var i=0; i<end; ++i) {
    ...
}
```

Comparison Operators

WMLScript provides the standard six comparison operators: *equal to* represented by ==, *not equal to* represented by !=, *less than* represented by <, *less than or equal to* represented by <=, *greater than* represented by >, and *greater than or equal to* represented by >=.

Expression the *equal to* comparison is the classic gotcha of C-like languages. You need to be careful to write == rather than = if you mean the "equal to" comparison operation. If by mistake you write:

```
if (a = b)
```

rather than:

```
if (a == b)
```

the result is still a valid WMLScript statement! However, rather than comparing a and b, it copies b into a and then tests if a can be converted to Boolean true. This can lead to some subtle bugs, so be careful.

These comparison operators all work by first checking if either operand is a string. If this is the case, they convert the other operand to a string and compare the two strings in dictionary order. Uppercase letters compare as less than lowercase, so "one" comes before "two", but "THREE" comes before "four". If one string is a prefix of another, the shorter one comes first, so "six" comes before "sixteen".

If neither operand is a string, the operators try to convert both operands to integers. If this works, the comparison is done on integers.

If the operands can't both be converted to integers, the operators try to convert them to floating point: if this works, the comparison is done on floating-point values.

If all the attempts fail (this is the case if one is invalid), the result of the comparison is invalid.

For example:

```
2 < 10 gives true (compared as integers)
"2" < 10 gives false (compared as strings: "2" < "10")
2.0 == 2 gives true (compared as floating point)
"six" > "seven" gives true (compared as strings)
true > false gives true (compared as integers: 1 > 0)
"true" > false gives true (compared as strings: "true" > "false")
```

Type Operators

By now, you've heard a lot about the different datatypes WMLScript provides and how it converts among these as necessary.

There are occasions where you may want to find the exact datatype of a value, or at the very least check whether it's invalid or not. (invalid usually represents some sort of error condition, so this last check is often equivalent to checking whether some operation went well.)

Fortunately, WMLScript provides operators for testing datatype and validity.

The `typeof` operator returns an integer representing the datatype of its argument. It doesn't attempt to do any conversions: the integer indicates the datatype of the argument.

Because the `typeof` operator never attempts to convert its argument and returns an integer value even when its argument is `invalid`, it never returns an `invalid` value. It always returns an integer.

Table 11-1 gives the five integer values that represent the five WMLScript datatypes.

Table 11-1. Values Given by typeof

Datatype	typeof Value
Integer	0
Floating point	1
String	2
Boolean	3
Invalid	4

Often, the `typeof` operator provides more information than you need. For example, consider a complicated arithmetic expression. You know that the result is either an integer or a floating-point value, unless something went wrong with the evaluation, in which case the result is `invalid`. You could check if everything went well with something like:

```
if (typeof result != 4) {
    /* Type not invalid: result was OK. */
    ...
} else {
    /* Type invalid: evaluation failed. */
    ...
}
```

WMLScript also provides a simpler operator, `isvalid`, which simply tests that a value isn't `invalid`. Just like `typeof`, it doesn't try to convert its value.

The last fragment could be written more efficiently using `isvalid`, without changing its behavior at all:

```
if (isvalid result) {
    /* Type not invalid: result was OK. */
    ...
} else {
    /* Type invalid: evaluation failed. */
    ...
}
```

For example:

```
typeof 0 gives 0
typeof 0.0 gives 1
typeof "" gives 2
typeof true gives 3
typeof invalid gives 4
typeof "0" gives 2
typeof "true" gives 2
typeof (17+1/0) gives 4
typeof (10/5) gives 1 (/ always gives a floating-point result)
```

The Conditional Operator

The conditional operator in WMLScript selects between two subexpressions depending on the result of a condition expression. Its syntax is:

```
condition-expression ? true-expression : false-expression
```

The *condition-expression* is converted to a Boolean value, and if this results in true the result is the *true-expression*, and the *false-expression* isn't evaluated. If the condition gives Boolean false or can't be converted, the result is the *false-expression*, and the *true-expression* isn't evaluated. Neither the *true-expression* nor the *false-expression* are converted in any way. The result of the conditional operator is of the same type as the selected subexpression.

Note that:

```
a = b ? c : d;
```

always has exactly the same effect as:

```
if (b) {
    a = c;
} else {
    a = d;
}
```

(Using the conditional operator is usually slightly more efficient than using if and else, however.)

For example:

```
true ? "yes" : "no" gives string "yes"
false ? "yes" : "no" gives string "no"
invalid ? "yes" : "no" gives string "no"
true ? 1/2 : 1/0 gives floating-point 0.5
false ? 1/2 : 1/0 gives invalid
true ? "" : foo() gives string "" and doesn't call foo()
```

Multiple Side Effects

The effect of an expression with multiple side effects to the same variable isn't explicitly defined in WMLScript. This includes the classic example:

```
x = x++
```

(Here, the variable **x** is incremented as a result of the **++** operator but is also assigned to by the **=** operator.)

Don't write code like this. Its behavior varies from browser to browser and from compiler to compiler. There is also no reason for doing it.

The Comma Operator

The **,** operator in WMLScript isn't used very often. Its effect is to evaluate its left operand, throw away the result, then evaluate its right operand. The result of the **,** operator is simply its right operand.

This behavior may seem bizarre if you haven't come across this operator before. It's used only when the left operand has some sort of side effect (such as an assignment to a variable or a function call). The most common use is in the initializer and increment sections of a **for** loop (see Chapter 12, *WMLScript Statements*). For example:

```
for (i=0, order=1, total=0; i<count; ++i, order *= 10) {
    total += foo (i, order);
}
```

In this loop, the initializer uses the **,** operator to initialize all three variables **i**, **order**, and **total**. In addition, the increment part uses the **,** operator not only to increment **i**, but also to multiply **order** by 10.

If the **,** operator is used in an argument to a function call or in a variable initializer, there can be some ambiguity. (Does the **,** represent the operator, or simply the comma before the next argument or variable declaration?) To avoid this, the whole expression containing the **,** must be parenthesized, but it's probably clearer to simply avoid using the **,** operator at all in these situations. Instead, simply add another statement. For example:

```
var x = foo(), bar();
```

is wrong, because there are no parentheses around the **,** expression. It should instead be written as:

```
var x = (foo (), bar ());
```

However, it's much clearer to write instead:

```
foo ();
var x = bar ();
```

Precedence and Associativity

Like most programming languages, WMLScript assigns a level of *precedence* to each of the operators. In addition, each binary operator has an *associativity*. These exist to disambiguate expressions without the need for lots of extra parentheses.

The precedence determines which parts of an expression are evaluated first when there are different operators involved. For example, the * operator has a higher precedence than the + operator, so:

```
3 + 4 * 5
```

is actually equivalent to:

```
3 + (4 * 5)
```

not:

```
(3 + 4) * 5
```

and the answer is 23, not 35.

Associativity determines which parts of an expression should be evaluated first when there are several operators of the same precedence together. (All operators of the same precedence always have the same associativity.) Associativity is specified as either *left* or *right*. Left-associative operators evaluate their left side first, and right-associative operators evaluate their right side first.

For example, + and – are both left-associative with the same precedence, so:

```
3 - 4 + 5
```

is equivalent to:

```
(3 - 4) + 5
```

rather than:

```
3 - (4 + 5)
```

and the answer is 4, not –6.

Similarly, the assignment operators are all right-associative with the same precedence, so:

```
a = b = c
```

is equivalent to:

```
a = (b = c)
```

rather than:

    (a = b) = c

which would not be legal, since:

    a = b

isn't a variable, so can't appear on the left side of the = operator.

Appendix C summarizes all the WMLScript operators, together with their precedence and associativity.

12

WMLScript Statements

This chapter covers WMLScript statements, which provide such useful control structures as loops and conditions, as well as simpler features such as the ability to return a value from a function.

Almost all of these features are similar to those found in languages such as C and Java, except that WMLScript doesn't provide quite the same rich selection. For example, there is no **switch** statement, and none of the extra statements found in Java are present in WMLScript.

This shouldn't be a problem, however. WMLScript was designed only for simple operations, such as checking that input is valid before sending it to the server. For anything complicated enough to need many more features, you'll probably be doing the real work on the server anyway.

Expressions as Statements

Any WMLScript expression can be turned into a statement by simply following it with a semicolon. This means that the expression is evaluated, but its result is thrown away. Any side effects of the expression still occur, however. The most common types of expressions to use as statements are the various assignments. (These are used far more often as statements than as expressions.)

For example:

```
a = b;
foo ();
x++;
total += value;
```

Blocks of Statements

Another simple type of statement is the block statement. This is simply a number of statements collected together and surrounded with curly braces. These are often used with `if` statements and `while` and `for` loops, to allow the parts of the `if` or the body of the loop to contain more than one statement.

For example:

```
{} is an empty block
{ a = b; } contains only one statement
{ a = b; foo (); bar (); } contains three statements
```

Conditions

Conditional statements in WMLScript behave just like they do in C. The simplest form looks like:

```
if (condition)
    statement-when-true
```

The *condition* is simply any expression. It's evaluated, and if the result can be converted to Boolean `true`, the *statement-when-true* is executed. For example:

```
if (x > max)
    max = x;
```

An `else` clause can also be added, looking like:

```
if (condition)
    statement-when-true
else
    statement-when-false
```

If the condition can be converted to Boolean `true`, *statement-when-true* is executed, but if the condition converts to Boolean `false` or can't be converted, *statement-when-false* is executed. For example:

```
if (number == 1)
    result = "1 apple";
else
    result = number + " apples";
```

Sometimes, the *statement-when-false* is itself another `if`. There is nothing special about this: the first *condition* is evaluated, and if it's `false` or can't be converted, the second `if` is executed. For example:

```
if (x > max)
    max = x;
else if (x < min)
    min = x;
```

Matters are more interesting if the *statement-when-true* contains an `if` with an `else` clause. For example, consider:

```
if (x)
    if (y)
        foo ();
    else
        bar ();
```

What exactly does this mean? The indentation suggests that the `else` belongs with the second `if`, but the compiler doesn't look at the indentation: all spaces are the same to it. The same code could equally be interpreted as:

```
if (x)
    if (y)
        foo ();
else
    bar ();
```

(That is, with the `else` attached to the first `if`.)

This ambiguity is known as the *dangling else problem* and affects many different programming languages. WMLScript resolves it by defining that any `else` belongs with the closest `if`. It's clearer, however, to avoid it altogether using curly braces to wrap the *statement-when-true* and *statement-when-false* into block statements, turning the last example into:

```
if (x) {
    if (y)
        foo ();
    else
        bar ();
}
```

Some people make a point of always putting curly braces around things, even if it's just a single statement. This is a useful way to make sure you get exactly what you expect.

Loops

As well as conditions with `if` and `else`, WMLScript provides looping constructs. There are two types: `for` and `while`. Both behave very much as they do in C.

A `while` loop executes its body while a condition is `true`. If the condition is `false` at the start, the body is never executed. (As with `if`, failure to convert to Boolean is taken as `false`.) It looks like:

```
while (condition)
    body
```

For example:

```
while (n > 1) {
    total *= n;
    --n;
}
```

A `for` loop is much more flexible and powerful. It looks like:

```
for (initializer; condition; increment)
    body
```

First, the optional *initializer* is evaluated as an expression. Instead of simply initializing a variable that was previously declared:

```
for (i=0; i<count; i++)
```

you can declare the variable in the initializer as well:

```
for (var i=0; i<count; i++)
```

The *body* is then executed while the *condition* can be converted to Boolean `true`. (As with `while`, if the *condition* isn't `true` at the start, the *body* never gets executed.) The *condition* may also be omitted, in which case it's taken as being always `true`, so the loop runs forever unless something happens in the body to stop it.

After each execution of the *body*, the *increment* expression is evaluated as an expression statement. As with the *initializer* and *condition*, it may be omitted, in which case it's simply ignored.

It's good style to use a `for` loop when the loop runs over a fixed set of values, such as a range of integers or for the elements in a list, with a single variable tracking your progress through the set. Set up the loop variable in the *initializer*, test it in the *condition*, and advance it to the next item in the *increment*. For example:

```
for (var i=0; i<4; ++i)
    foo (i);
```

Here, i takes on the values 0, 1, 2, 3 in order. Note also the use of a variable declaration in the *initializer*.

There are two reasons for using `for` loops for these cases: first, they're clearer, and it's always good style to be clearer. The other reason is subtler and relates to the `continue` statement, which will be explained later in this chapter.

The break Statement

The `break` statement can appear in the body of any loop. It looks like this:

```
break;
```

If executed, it jumps right out of the loop, to the code following it. It's often used when an extra condition is detected in the middle of the loop, which means that the loop must stop. For example, a loop to search for a free entry can look like this:

```
var free_entry = -1;
for (var i=0; i<last; ++i) {
    if (entry_is_free (i)) {
        free_entry = i;
        break;
    }
}
```

If an entry is found, this sets the **free_entry** variable and exits the loop immediately.

The continue Statement

The **continue** statement also controls the behavior of loops, but rather than stopping the loop, it simply skips the rest of the current iteration and continues with the next one. It looks like this:

```
continue;
```

For a **while** loop, it simply jumps to the end of the body. The next action is to evaluate the condition again, to decide whether or not the loop is now finished.

In a **for** loop, executing a **continue** statement executes the **increment** part of the loop before retesting the condition. This means that if you use the initializer, condition, and increment to step through a set of values, executing a **continue** simply skips to the next value. For example:

```
for (var i=0; i<count; ++i) {
    if (i == 5)
        continue;

    do_something ();
}
```

Returning from a Function

The **return** statement ends execution of the current function. It has two forms:

```
return;
```

and:

```
return expression;
```

The first form (without an **expression**) is equivalent to:

```
return "";
```

Executing a **return** statement stops the current function immediately and returns the value of *expression* to the statement containing the function call. For example, you can check for an error condition at the top of a function and return **invalid**:

```
if (x < 0)
    return invalid;
```

Other Statements

Variable declarations with **var** are considered statements in WMLScript; so they can appear anywhere that a statement can. You don't have to stick them all at the top of a function as you do in some languages. For example:

```
foo ();
var x = 0105;
bar (x);
```

Sometimes, you want a statement that doesn't do anything. You can do this with an empty block, {}, but you can also simply use a single semicolon, which is a statement that does nothing. For example:

```
while (test_value (++x)) {
    /* Empty block. */
}
```

or:

```
while (test_value (++x))
    ;
```

Writing loops like this, with all of the work crammed into the loop header, is often regarded as bad style; it can make your code hard to read.

13

WMLScript Functions

You've now seen nearly all the elements that make up WMLScript, but one thing that hasn't yet been properly covered is how you wrap these bits up into functions that can be called from WML.

That process is covered in this chapter, together with how you can put commonly used WMLScript functions into a single library and call these from different places.

Function Declarations

You've already seen examples of a function declaration—in Chapter 9, *Introduction to WMLScript*, and Chapter 10, *WMLScript Datatypes, Variables, and Conversions*—but you haven't seen all the details.

Functions are declared after any pragmas (more on pragmas in Chapter 14, *WMLScript Pragmas*). A function declaration looks like either:

```
function function-name (parameter-list)
{
    body
}
```

or:

```
extern function function-name (parameter-list)
{
    body
}
```

If the function is declared **extern**, it's available to be called from WML or from other WMLScript functions not declared in the same file. If it's declared without the **extern** keyword, it can be called only by other WMLScript code in the same source file.

The function name follows the same rules as WMLScript variable names: anything that is a legal variable name is a valid function name. In addition, you can use the same name for a variable and a function, since WMLScript keeps separate namespaces for each.

The function body is simply a list of WMLScript statements.

The *parameter-list* is a list of the names of each of the parameters to the function. These names follow the same rules as variable names. This is not surprising, since in the function body the parameters themselves behave exactly like variables. You reference them as though they were variables, and you can even change their values.

For example, here is a function that takes three parameters, named a, b, and c. It multiplies them and returns the result:

```
function multiply3 (a, b, c)
{
    return a * b * c;
}
```

As a more complicated example, here is a slight variant on the function for calculating factorials given in Chapter 9. This version uses the parameter n directly as the loop counter variable, rather than using a separate variable, showing how the parameters all behave exactly like variables:

```
function factorial (n)
{
    if (n < 0)
        return invalid;

    var total = 1;
    for (; n>1; --n) {
        total *= n;
    }
    return total;
}
```

This can also be written using a **while** loop:

```
function factorial (n)
{
    if (n < 0)
        return invalid;

    var total = 1;
    while (n > 1) {
        total *= n;
        --n;
    }
    return total;
}
```

Note that just like the rest of WMLScript, you don't specify the datatype of the function result. In fact, a function can even return values of different types (just as the previous example does: it returns either an integer or `invalid`).

There is also no way to specify a function that doesn't return a value: all functions return something. However, a function doesn't have to have a `return` statement, and a `return` statement doesn't have to have a value. In both of these cases, the function returns an empty string.

Function Calls

Function calls in WMLScript look just like they do in C or Java:

```
function-name (argument-list)
```

The number of arguments supplied to the function must match the number of arguments in its declaration. The arguments can be any expressions, but if any of them contain the , operator, that whole argument must be enclosed in parentheses. (Otherwise, there would be ambiguity as to whether it was the , operator or just a comma separating two arguments.) For example:

```
factorial (5)
foo ()
function_with_lots_of_arguments (1, 2, 3, 4, 5, 6, 7, 8, 9)
```

Note that this form of function call works only for calls within the same file. Calls to functions in other files use an extended syntax.

Calls to Other Script Units

To call a function in another file, you must specify the external file in the call:

```
file-identifier#function-name (argument-list)
```

The function name and argument list are the same as before. The *file-identifier* references a URL via a name set up with a `url` pragma. (This pragma is described in the next section.) The *file-identifier* name itself follows the same rules as variable names. Examples of external function calls include:

```
mathlibrary#factorial (6)
arraylibrary#sort (array)
netlib#check_email_address (addr)
```

The url pragma

The `url` pragma that names the external file looks like this:

```
use url file-identifier url-string;
```

The *file-identifier* is the name used in the external function calls. It follows the same rules as variable names. You can have a *file-identifier* with the same name as either a WMLScript function or a variable, because all three use different namespaces.

The *url-string* is a normal WMLScript string literal. Its contents must be a valid URL. This URL may be relative or absolute: relative URLs are *resolved* against the URL used to fetch the current script module. (URL resolving is discussed in Appendix A, *Absolute and Relative URLs*.) This URL must not contain a # character, so it can't specify a fragment.

Here are some examples:

```
use url netlib "http://wap.net/lib/netlib.wmlsc";
use url test "test.wmlsc";
use url example "/script/example.wmlsc";
```

Calling WMLScript from WML

At last, here's the part that tells you how to actually get the browser to call all this WMLScript you've been writing!

A function to be called from WML must be declared **extern**. However, there are no other restrictions on it. It can have as many arguments as you like, and these arguments can be of any type.

Embedding the Function Call in a <go> Task

You call WMLScript from WML by using a <go> task with a specially formatted URL. The function to call and the arguments to pass are encoded into the URL fragment (the part after the first # character). This fragment looks just like a normal WMLScript function call. For example, a call to the function **test('foo')** in the file referenced by the relative URL **test.wmlsc** can be written as:

```
<go href="test.wmlsc#test('foo')"/>
```

Note that this uses single quotes around the string **'foo'**. It can be equally well written as:

```
<go href='test.wmlsc#test("foo")'/>
```

It's probably best to be consistent about using either single or double quotes around all your attribute values and then use the other kind around any strings in the embedded call to WMLScript. For example, I always put double quotes around attribute values, and then always use single quotes around embedded strings, just like the first form of the last call.

The following sections describe differences between how you embed a WML-
Script call in a <go> task's URL and how you would write the call in WMLScript
itself.

Variable substitution

Because the call is embedded in a normal WML <go> task, you can do all the
things you can with a WML task, including substituting browser variables directly
into the call. For example, to change the last function call to pass the value of the
variable var instead of the fixed string 'foo', you can write:

```
<go href="test.wmlsc#test('$(var:n)')"/>
```

The :n forces the variable to be substituted without URL-escaping.

Note that you still need to put the quotes around the argument string. This is
because, as always, the browser does the variable substitution before it has even
noticed that the task is actually a call to WMLScript. If you don't put the quotes in,
the browser tries to interpret the value as some other type of literal (integer, boolean, or floating point).

Because the variable substitution is done before the call is parsed, you can even
substitute the entire function call part of the URL. For example, if the variable
call contained the value test('foo'), you can write:

```
<go href="test.wmlsc#$(call:n)"/>
```

and it has exactly the same effect as the first example.

No expressions as arguments in shorthand forms of the <go> task

Another feature of using a normal <go> task is that you can use the shorthand
forms provided by some WML constructs, such as event bindings. For example,
you can have a function called when a WML timer expires using this event binding:

```
<onevent type="ontimer">
    <go href="process.wmlsc#timeout()"/>
</onevent)
```

This can be shortened to a single attribute on the <card> element:

```
ontimer="process.wmlsc#timeout()"
```

The WMLScript call embedded in a <go> task's URL can't contain any expressions:
all the arguments have to be literal values after the browser has performed variable substitution. (The one exception: you can use unary minus to specify negative numbers.) This isn't a problem, however: you can simply pass all the "raw"
values to the function and implement the expression inside the function.

For example, if you want to call the function **foo()** in *example.wmlsc* with the sum of the two browser variables **var_a** and **var_b**, you can't just write:

```
<go href="example.wmlsc#foo($(var_a:n)+$(var_b:n))"/>
```

because the argument is not a literal value. Instead, rewrite the function to accept both the browser variables:

```
<go href="example.wmlsc#foo($(var_a:n),$(var_b:n)"/>
```

and have the WMLScript function **foo()** perform the addition.

Alternatively, you can perform the addition in a "wrapper" function, and then pass the result to the original, single-argument version of **foo()**:

```
extern function foo_wrapper (a, b)
{
    foo (a + b);
}
```

In this case, the call is:

```
<go href="example.wmlsc#foo_wrapper($(var_a:n),$(var_b:n)"/>
```

Additional minor differences

A WMLScript function call embedded in a URL can't have spaces between the function name and the opening (of the argument list.

String constants can't contain any escape sequences* such as **\n**, **\0243**, or **\0xAD**. They aren't often necessary, as you can get nearly the same effect with WML character entities (such as **
** for a newline). The only things you can't do with entities are putting a single quote into a string quoted with single quotes, or a double quote into a string quoted with double quotes. There is no easy way around this restriction.

Examples of Calling WMLScript from WML

To summarize, here are some tasks calling WMLScript from WML:

```
<go href="netlib.wmlsc#check_email('$(email)')"/>
<go href="http://wap.net/foo.wmlsc#foo()"/>
<go href="example.wmlsc#use_string('foo')"/>
<go href="example.wmlsc#use_integer(17)"/>
<go href="example.wmlsc#use_integer(0105)"/>
<go href="example.wmlsc#use_integer(0x3e8)"/>
<go href="example.wmlsc#use_float(.01)"/>
<go href="example.wmlsc#use_float(1e-2)"/>
<go href="example.wmlsc#use_boolean(true)"/>
```

---

* In fact, in the now obsolete WAP 1.0 specifications, string literals *could* contain escape sequences like these. This feature was removed in the WAP 1.1 documents.

```
<go href="example.wmlsc#use_boolean(false)"/>
<go href="example.wmlsc#use_invalid(invalid)"/>
```

Standard Libraries

If you find yourself regularly using the same functions in different WMLScript code, you can put them into a library. Simply put them all in the same file and declare them all extern. They can then be accessed from all your WMLScript code using a url pragma and an external function call, as described earlier in this chapter.

In addition to these user-defined libraries, WMLScript provides libraries that are built into the browser itself, not written in WMLScript. They can do tasks no program written purely in WMLScript can do. (Think of these as being a bit like system calls in a normal programming language.) These libraries are called *standard libraries*, to differentiate them from user-defined libraries written in WMLScript.

Because WMLScript is designed for simplicity, there are a number of useful things it simply can't do directly. For example, although it can concatenate strings (using the + operator), there's no way to then take substrings, extract single characters from the string, or do any of the other common operations that you might want to do to your strings, and that all other programming languages allow you to do.

Similarly, there's no consistent way to convert values between the different datatypes. Yes, the values are converted automatically if required, but the problems with the + operator mentioned in Chapter 11, *WMLScript Operators and Expressions*, show how it can sometimes be important to force a value to a particular datatype.

All these functions and more are provided in WMLScript's standard libraries. Because they are built into the browser, they don't have to be downloaded every time, so using them helps keep the size of your code down.

Calling the Standard Libraries

All standard libraries are called in the same way, with an extension to the normal syntax for WMLScript function calls:

    library-name.function-name (argument-list)

The names of both the library and the function are fixed by the implementor of the library. You can't choose these: you need to know what they are before you can use the library. The six libraries from the official specifications are described in Chapters 15 through 20.

Individual browser implementations may include additional standard libraries. These vendor-specific libraries must be supported by both the device and the compiler to be used. If a specific device supports vendor-specific libraries, you have to consult the vendor's own documentation to find out the details of the functions. However, they can still be called using this standard syntax.

The `argument-list` is simply a list of expressions, just as with normal function calls.

14

WMLScript Pragmas

This chapter discusses the features of WMLScript known as *pragmas*, which specify meta-information about a WMLScript unit, in a similar way to the <meta> and <access> elements for WML files. (See Chapter 6, *WML Decks, Templates, and Cards*, for more information on these WML elements.)

You have already encountered one pragma, the url pragma for referencing other WMLScript units, in Chapter 13, *WMLScript Functions*. In addition, there is an access pragma, corresponding to WML's <access> element, and a meta pragma, corresponding to the <meta> element. These pragmas are processed by the WAP gateway (see Appendix B, *WAP Gateways and WSP*) to control the headers sent along with the compiled unit.

All pragmas in a WMLScript file must be specified before any functions. The individual pragmas may be specified in any order, however.

The access Pragma

The access pragma provides the same simple access control as the <access> element does for WML decks. That is, it specifies a domain and path that must match the URL of the caller for a call to be permitted.

There are three forms:

```
use access domain domain;
use access path path;
use access domain domain path path;
```

Both *domain* and *path* are normal WMLScript string literals. They are interpreted in exactly the same way as the domain and path attributes of WML's <access>

element. (See Chapter 6 for more information.) There may be no more than one `access` pragma per WMLScript file.

For example, the pragma:

```
use access domain "wap.net" path "/private";
```

restricts access to WML and WMLScript that originates from the `/private` area of a server in the *wap.net* domain.

The meta Pragma

The `meta` pragma allows arbitrary meta-information to be included in a WML deck. There are three variations on it:

```
use meta name name value scheme;
use meta http equiv name value scheme;
use meta user agent name value scheme;
```

In all cases, the three parameters *name*, *value*, and *scheme* are all normal WML-Script string literals. The *name* parameter specifies a property name, and *value* specifies its value. The *scheme* parameter is optional: it specifies how the property is to be interpreted. It's not used by anything defined in the official standards but might be used in some implementation-specific way.

The interpretation of the meta-information depends on the form used:

`meta name`

> Meta-information specified with this form is for the origin server's use only. It isn't transmitted to the client. For example:
>
> ```
> use meta name "last-modified" "2000-05-15";
> ```

`meta http equiv`

> Specifies an HTTP or WSP header to be sent along with this WMLScript file. This can specify how the file should be cached and many other things. For example:
>
> ```
> use meta http equiv "cache-control" "no-cache";
> ```

`meta user agent`

> Specifies a property that is passed to the WMLScript interpreter. It's up to the browser to decide what to do with it. No specific property names are officially defined. If a particular browser supports such information, you need to consult its documentation to find the names of the properties and what their values should be. For example:
>
> ```
> use meta user agent "x-debugging" "on";
> ```

15

The Lang Library

The Lang standard library contains simple functions that extend the core functionality of WMLScript. This includes functions for explicitly converting strings to integers and floating-point numbers, for generating random numbers, and for determining various constants related to the WMLScript interpreter.

---

abort   Stop execution of WMLScript interpreter (due to an error)

Usage

Lang.abort(*msg*)   *msg* : String

Description

Aborts the WMLScript interpreter, displays the message string *msg*, and returns control to whatever caused the interpreter to be run (such as the WML browser). This function never returns to the WMLScript code.

If *msg* is invalid, it's converted to the string "invalid".

Example

Lang.abort("fatal error: bad arguments")

---

abs   Return the absolute value of a number

Usage

Lang.abs(*num*)   *num* : Number

Description

If *num* is an integer or can be converted to one, returns a positive integer. Otherwise, if *num* is a floating-point value or can be converted to one, returns a positive floating-point value.

114

Examples

`Lang.abs(17)`	returns integer 17
`Lang.abs("-17")`	returns integer 17
`Lang.abs(2.3)`	returns floating-point 2.3
`Lang.abs(-2.3)`	returns floating-point 2.3
`Lang.abs("foo")`	returns `invalid`

---

characterSet

Return the identifier for the character set supported by the WMLScript interpreter

Usage

`Lang.characterSet()`

Description

The WMLScript specification requires the interpreter to use a single character set internally. All strings in code to be executed must be converted to this single character set, which is used for determining the order of characters when comparing strings.

This function returns the *MIBenum* of this character set. This is an integer value defined by the Internet Assigned Numbers Authority (IANA). The list of all assigned MIBenum values can be found at *ftp://ftp.isi.edu/in-notes/iana/assignments/character-sets*.

Example

`Lang.characterSet()`   can return 1000, meaning Unicode

---

exit

Stop execution of the WMLScript interpreter (normal)

Usage

`Lang.exit(value)`   *value* : Anything

Description

Exits from the WMLScript interpreter and returns *value* to whatever caused the interpreter to be run (such as the WML browser). This function never returns to the WMLScript code.

If WMLScript is invoked from WML, as is currently the only way, this exit value is ignored.

Examples

```
Lang.exit("foo")
Lang.exit(invalid)
Lang.exit(6.7)
```

---

float

Report whether the interpreter supports floating-point operations

Usage

`Lang.float()`

Description

Returns `true` if this interpreter supports floating-point operations; returns `false` otherwise.

Example

```
Lang.float()
```
                                    returns either Boolean `true` or Boolean
                                    `false`

---

isFloat   Test whether a string can be parsed as a floating-point value

Usage

```
Lang.isFloat(str)
```
                                    str : String

Description

Returns `true` or `false`, depending on whether *str* can be parsed as a floating-point value by `Lang.parseFloat()`.

Returns `invalid` if *str* can't be converted to a string or if the interpreter doesn't support floating-point operations.

Examples

```
Lang.isFloat("123.456")
Lang.isFloat("17")
Lang.isFloat(" -7.2 C")
Lang.isFloat(" 55.3 mph")
Lang.isFloat("6e+3")
Lang.isFloat(" .3")
Lang.isFloat("foo")
Lang.isFloat(false)
Lang.isFloat(invalid)
```
                                    returns Boolean `true`
                                    returns Boolean `true`
                                    returns Boolean `true`
                                    returns Boolean `true`
                                    returns Boolean `true`
                                    returns Boolean `true`
                                    returns Boolean `false`
                                    returns Boolean `false`
                                    returns `invalid`

---

isInt   Test whether a string can be parsed as an integer

Usage

```
Lang.isInt(str)
```
                                    str : String

Description

Returns `true` or `false`, depending on whether *str* can be parsed as an integer by `Lang.parseInt()`. Returns `invalid` if *str* can't be converted to a string.

Examples

```
Lang.isInt("17")
Lang.isInt("23.67")
Lang.isInt(" -63 percent")
Lang.isInt("+4inches")
Lang.isInt(true)
Lang.isInt(".3")
```
                                    returns Boolean `true`
                                    returns Boolean `true`
                                    returns Boolean `true`
                                    returns Boolean `true`
                                    returns Boolean `false`
                                    returns Boolean `false`

`Lang.isInt("+")`	returns Boolean `false`
`Lang.isInt(invalid)`	returns `invalid`

max
Return the larger of two numbers

Usage

`Lang.max(num1, num2)`	*num1* : Number
	num2 : Number

Description

Returns the larger of *num1* and *num2*. If they are equal, returns *num1*. The value returned has the same type as the operand.

If either *num1* or *num2* can't be converted to a number, returns `invalid`.

Examples

`Lang.max(-2, 3.4)`	returns floating-point `3.4`
`Lang.max(17, 23)`	returns integer `23`
`Lang.max(-3, -3.0)`	returns integer `-3`
`Lang.max(-5, false)`	returns Boolean `false`
`Lang.max("6", 6)`	returns string `"6"`
`Lang.max("six", 6)`	returns `invalid`

maxInt
Return the largest supported integer value

Usage

`Lang.maxInt()`

Description

Always returns the same integer value, the largest value that the WMLScript interpreter can process.

Example

`Lang.maxInt()`	returns integer `2147483647`

min
Return the smaller of two numbers

Usage

`Lang.min(num1, num2)`	*num1* : Number
	num2 : Number

Description

Returns the smaller of *num1* and *num2*. If they are equal, returns *num1*. The value returned has the same type as the operand.

If either *num1* or *num2* can't be converted to a number, returns `invalid`.

Examples

`Lang.min(1, -2.0)`	returns floating-point `-2.0`
`Lang.min(17, 23)`	returns integer `17`
`Lang.min(4.0, 4)`	returns floating-point `4.0`
`Lang.min(true, 2)`	returns Boolean `true`
`Lang.min("-1", -1)`	returns string `"-1"`
`Lang.min(42, "foo")`	returns `invalid`

---

minInt   Return the smallest supported integer value

Usage

`Lang.minInt()`

Description

Always returns the same integer value, the smallest (most negative) value that the WMLScript interpreter can process.

Example

`Lang.minInt()`   returns integer `-2147483648`

---

parseFloat   Convert a string to a floating-point value

Usage

`Lang.parseFloat(str)`   *str* : String

Description

Attempts to parse the string *str* as a floating-point literal. A leading + or – may be included; any spaces at the start of the string are ignored, as are any characters at the end that can't be parsed as part of the number.

Returns `invalid` if *str* can't be parsed as a floating-point value, or if the interpreter doesn't support floating-point operations.

Examples

`Lang.parseFloat("123.456")`	returns floating-point `123.456`
`Lang.parseFloat("17")`	returns floating-point `17.0`
`Lang.parseFloat(" -7.2 C")`	returns floating-point `7.2`
`Lang.parseFloat(" 55.3 mph")`	returns floating-point `55.3`
`Lang.parseFloat("6e+3")`	returns floating-point `6000.0`
`Lang.parseFloat(" .3")`	returns floating-point `0.3`
`Lang.parseFloat("foo")`	returns `invalid`
`Lang.parseFloat(false)`	returns `invalid`

parseInt   Convert a string to an integer

Usage

`Lang.parseInt(str)`   *str* : String

Description

Attempts to parse the string *str* as a decimal integer. A leading + or – may be included; any spaces at the start of the string are ignored, as are any characters at the end that can't be parsed as part of the integer.

If *str* can't be parsed as an integer, returns `invalid`.

Examples

`Lang.parseInt("17")`	returns integer 17
`Lang.parseInt("23.67")`	returns integer 23
`Lang.parseInt(" -63 percent")`	returns integer –63
`Lang.parseInt("+4inches")`	returns integer 4
`Lang.parseInt(true)`	returns `invalid`
`Lang.parseInt(".3")`	returns `invalid`
`Lang.parseInt("+")`	returns `invalid`

random   Generate a random integer

Usage

`Lang.random(range)`   *range* : Number

Description

Returns a random integer that is greater than or equal to zero, and less than or equal to *range*. If *range* is a floating-point value, `Float.int()` converts it to an integer first.

The random values are approximately uniformly distributed over the full range, but they shouldn't be relied on if security is important.

If *range* is zero, returns zero; if *range* is less than zero, returns `invalid`.

Examples

`Lang.random(23)`	returns an integer between 0 and 23 inclusive
`Lang.random(17.2)`	returns an integer between 0 and 17 inclusive
`Lang.random("foo")`	returns `invalid`

seed   Set the seed value for the random number generator

Usage

`Lang.seed(seed)`   *seed* : Number

Description

Seeds the random number generator used by `Lang.random()`. If *seed* is less than zero, uses a random internal value (typically, the system time). Otherwise, uses *seed* to seed the generator. If *seed* is a floating-point value, `Float.int()` first converts it to an integer.

Returns the empty string; but if *seed* can't be converted to a number, returns `invalid`.

Examples

`Lang.seed(23)`	seeds with integer 23 and returns `""`
`Lang.seed(1.2)`	seeds with integer 1 and returns `""`
`Lang.seed("foo")`	returns `invalid` and doesn't change the seed.

16

The Float Library

The `Float` standard library contains functions for operating on floating-point numbers, including simple operations for converting to integers, as well as more complicated functions such as square root.

Some WMLScript interpreters don't support floating-point operations at all. If this is the case, all functions in this library return `invalid`, regardless of their arguments.

---

ceil   Return the ceiling of a floating-point value

Usage

`Float.ceil(num)`   *num* : Floating point

Description

Returns the smallest integer value that is less than or equal to *num*. Returns *num* itself if it's an integer. Returns `invalid` if *num* can't be converted to floating point or if the result won't fit into an integer.

Examples

`Float.ceil(17.0)`	returns integer 17
`Float.ceil(17.4)`	returns integer 18
`Float.ceil(17.5)`	returns integer 18
`Float.ceil(-17.0)`	returns integer –17
`Float.ceil(-17.4)`	returns integer –17
`Float.ceil(-17.5)`	returns integer –17
`Float.ceil(5e10)`	returns `invalid`
`Float.ceil(-5e10)`	returns `invalid`
`Float.ceil("foo")`	returns `invalid`

floor
Return the floor of a floating-point value

Usage

`Float.floor(num)`   *num* : Floating point

Description

Returns the largest integer value that is less than or equal to *num*. Returns *num* itself if it's an integer. Returns `invalid` if *num* can't be converted to floating point or if the result won't fit into an integer.

Examples

`Float.floor(17.0)`	returns integer `17`
`Float.floor(17.4)`	returns integer `17`
`Float.floor(17.5)`	returns integer `17`
`Float.floor(-17.0)`	returns integer `-17`
`Float.floor(-17.4)`	returns integer `-18`
`Float.floor(-17.5)`	returns integer `-18`
`Float.floor(5e10)`	returns `invalid`
`Float.floor(-5e10)`	returns `invalid`
`Float.floor("foo")`	returns `invalid`

int
Truncate a floating-point value to an integer

Usage

`Float.int(num)`   *num* : Floating point

Description

Returns an integer value formed by ignoring everything after the decimal point. Returns *num* itself if it's an integer. Returns `invalid` if *num* can't be converted to floating point or if the result won't fit into an integer.

Examples

`Float.int(17.0)`	returns integer `17`
`Float.int(17.4)`	returns integer `17`
`Float.int(17.5)`	returns integer `17`
`Float.int(-17.0)`	returns integer `-17`
`Float.int(-17.4)`	returns integer `-17`
`Float.int(-17.5)`	returns integer `-17`
`Float.int(5e10)`	returns `invalid`
`Float.int(-5e10)`	returns `invalid`
`Float.int("foo")`	returns `invalid`

---

maxFloat
Return the largest supported floating-point value

Usage

`Float.maxFloat()`

Description

Always returns the same value, the largest supported floating-point value.

Example

`Float.maxFloat()`   might return `3.40282347e38`

---

minFloat
Return the minimum supported positive floating-point value

Usage

`Float.minFloat()`

Description

Always returns the same value, the smallest supported positive floating-point value.

The exact value varies from implementation to implementation. Some return the smallest normalized value (the smallest value that can be represented without losing precision); others return the smallest possible value (where precision is lost but there really is no number smaller).

This ambiguity is permitted by the specification of this function: the only thing guaranteed is that the value is less than or equal to the smallest normalized positive floating-point value, which is 1.17549435e-38 for WMLScript.

Example

`Float.minFloat()`   returns a floating-point number less than or equal to `1.17549435e-38`

---

pow
Raise a number to a power

Usage

`Float.pow(base, power)`   *base*: Floating point
power: Floating point

Description

Returns the result of raising *base* to the power *power*. This result may be approximate with some WMLScript interpreters.

There are two special restrictions that come from mathematical properties of raising numbers to powers: if *base* is negative, *power* must be an integer, and if *base* is zero, *power* must not be negative. If either of these conditions isn't met, returns `invalid`.

Examples

Float.pow(3.0, 2.0)	returns floating-point 9.0
Float.pow(9.0, 0.5)	returns floating-point 3.0
Float.pow(8.0, 1/3)	returns floating-point 2.0
Float.pow(-2.0, 0.0)	returns floating-point 1.0
Float.pow(-2.0, 4.0)	returns floating-point 16.0
Float.pow(-2.0, 5.0)	returns floating-point -32.0
Float.pow(-2.0, -1.0)	returns floating-point -0.5
Float.pow(-2.0, 0.5)	returns invalid
Float.pow(0.0, 1.7)	returns floating-point 0.0
Float.pow(0.0, 0.0)	returns floating-point 1.0
Float.pow(0.0, -1.0)	returns invalid
Float.pow(1e20, 2.0)	returns invalid

---

round   Round a floating-point value to the nearest integer

Usage

Float.round(*num*)   *num* : Floating point

Description

Returns the closest integer to *num*. Returns *num* itself if it's an integer. Values ending in .5 are defined to be closest to the integer above.

Returns invalid if *num* can't be converted to floating point or if the result doesn't fit into an integer.

Examples

Float.round(17.0)	returns integer 17
Float.round(17.4)	returns integer 17
Float.round(17.5)	returns integer 18
Float.round(-17.0)	returns integer -17
Float.round(-17.4)	returns integer -17
Float.round(-17.5)	returns integer -17 (not -18)
Float.round(5e10)	returns invalid
Float.round(-5e10)	returns invalid
Float.round("foo")	returns invalid

---

sqrt   Return the square root of a number

Usage

Float.sqrt(*num*)   *num* : Floating point

Description

Returns the square root of *num*. Some WMLScript interpreters return only an approximation. Returns invalid if *num* can't be converted to floating point or if *num* is negative.

Examples

`Float.sqrt(4.0)`	returns floating-point `2.0`
`Float.sqrt(1.0)`	returns floating-point `1.0`
`Float.sqrt(0.0)`	returns floating-point `0.0`
`Float.sqrt(-1.0)`	returns `invalid`

17

The String Library

The `String` standard library contains routines for string manipulation. This includes functions for extracting individual characters from strings, for finding the lengths of strings, and also for treating strings as arrays of values and operating on them on this basis.

It's important to note that none of these functions actually changes the strings passed as arguments. Functions that claim to modify strings simply return a new string with the modification. The original is always unchanged.

---

charAt   Return the character at a given position in a string

Usage

```
String.charAt(str, index)
```
                                              str : String
                                              index : Number

Description

Extracts the single character at the specified *index* from the string *str*, and returns it as a single-character string. (The first character in the string has index zero.) If index is a floating-point number, it's converted to an integer with `Float.int()` before being used. If *index* is out of range (less than zero or past the end of the string), the empty string is returned.

If the arguments can't be converted to the correct types, `invalid` is returned.

Examples

```
String.charAt("Example", 0)          returns string "E"
String.charAt("Example", 3)          returns string "m"
String.charAt("Example", 6)          returns string "e"
String.charAt("Example", 7)          returns string ""
String.charAt "Example", -1)         returns string ""
```

```
String.charAt(42, 1)              returns string "2"
String.charAt(false, 4)          returns string "e"
String.charAt(invalid, 0)        returns invalid
String.charAt("foo", "bar")      returns invalid
```

compare
Compare two strings

Usage

```
String.compare(str1, str2)       str1 : String
                                 str2 : String
```

Description

Compares two strings lexicographically. Returns −1 if *str1* is less than *str2*, 1 if *str1* is greater than *str2*, and 0 if they are equal. If one string is a prefix of the other, the shorter string is the lesser one.

Returns invalid if either argument can't be converted to a string.

Examples

```
String.compare("one", "two")        returns integer −1
String.compare("two", "three")      returns integer 1
String.compare("four", "four")      returns integer 0
String.compare("six", "sixteen")    returns integer −1
String.compare(6, 16)               returns integer 1
String.compare(invalid, "foo")      returns invalid
String.compare("foo", invalid)      returns invalid
```

elementAt
Return a single item from a list that is stored as a string

Usage

```
String.elementAt(str, index, sep)    str : String
                                     index : Number
                                     sep : String
```

Description

This function processes a string as a list of string values, separated by a specified character (for example: `"first string|second|last, final one"`.)

The first character of *sep* is used as the separator; *str* is the string that is processed as a list of strings. The function returns the list item ("element") specified by *index*. (The first element has index zero.)

If *index* is past the end of the list of elements, the last element is returned. Similarly, if *index* is less than zero, the first element is returned. If *index* is a floating-point value, it's first converted to an integer with `Float.int()`. Note that an empty *str* is a valid list containing a single element: the empty string.

Returns invalid if any of the arguments can't be converted to the appropriate types or if *sep* is the empty string.

Examples

```
String.elementAt("a;b;c;d", 2, ";")        returns string "c"
String.elementAt("a;b;c;d", 23, ";")       returns string "d"
String.elementAt("a;b;c;d", -1, ";")       returns string "a"
String.elementAt("a;b;c;d", 1.3, ";")      returns string "b"
String.elementAt("", 1, "x")               returns string ""
String.elementAt(invalid, 1, "x")          returns invalid
String.elementAt("foo", "one", "x")        returns invalid
String.elementAt("foo", 1, invalid)        returns invalid
String.elementAt("foo", 1, "")             returns invalid
```

---

elements

Return the number of items in a list that is stored as a string

Usage

```
String.elements(str, sep)
```
str : String

sep : String

Description

(See `elementAt()`'s description for an explanation of how a string is processed as a list of "elements.")

Returns the number of elements in *str*. Note that an empty *str* is a valid list containing a single element: the empty string.

Returns `invalid` if either *str* or *sep* can't be converted to a string or if *sep* is the empty string.

Examples

```
String.elements("1;2;3;4", ";")            returns integer 4
String.elements("1;2;3;4", ";foo")         returns integer 4
String.elements("aa bbb c dd e", " ")      returns integer 5
String.elements("x,,y,,,,z", ",")          returns integer 7
String.elements("", "x")                   returns integer 1
String.elements("foo", "")                 returns invalid
String.elements(invalid, "x")              returns invalid
String.elements("foo", invalid)            returns invalid
```

---

find

Find a substring in a string

Usage

```
String.find(str, substr)
```
str : String

substr : String

Description

Returns the index of the first instance of substring *substr* in the string *str*. The first character in the string has index zero. Returns –1 if there is no occurrence of *substr* in *str*.

Returns `invalid` if either *str* or *substr* can't be converted to a string.

Examples

```
String.find("Example", "x")          returns integer 1
String.find("Example", "mp")         returns integer 3
String.find("Example", "plf")        returns integer -1
String.find("abababab", "baba")      returns integer 1
String.find(123456, 45)              returns integer 3
String.find(invalid, "foo")          returns invalid
String.find("foo", invalid)          returns invalid
```

---

format
Convert a value into a string with control over the formatting

Usage

```
String.format(format, value)
```
format : String
value : Anything

Description

Returns a string containing *value* converted to a string under the control of the *format* string. The behavior of *format* is similar to the format string for the C language `printf()` function, but it's simplified.

The *format* string can contain any characters and one *format specifier*, which is replaced with the converted *value* in the result. There are three variants of the format specifier, and in all cases any part inside *[]* may be omitted:

%[width][.max]s
Formats a string value: *value* is converted to a string with the normal WMLScript conversion rules. If *max* is specified, no more than that many characters from the string are included in the result. If *width* is specified, and the formatted part of the string has fewer than that many characters, it's padded on the left with spaces.

%[width][.digits]d
Formats a decimal integer value: *value* is converted to an integer with the normal WMLScript conversion rules. If *digits* is specified and the number has fewer than that many digits, it's padded with zeros. If *max* is specified as zero, and *value* is zero, the result is an empty string. After this, if *width* is specified, and the value still has fewer than that many characters, it's padded on the left with spaces.

%[width][.digits]f
Formats a floating-point value: *value* is converted to floating-point with the normal WMLScript conversion rules. If *digits* is specified, it specifies the number of digits to follow the decimal point: the part after the decimal point is formatted with exactly this many digits, truncating the value or padding on the right with zeros as necessary. If *digits* is specified as zero, or if the . character appears with no digits following, no decimal point is included. If *digits* isn't specified, it defaults to six digits. After this, if *width* is specified, and the value has fewer than that many characters, it's padded on the left with spaces.

If there's more than one format specifier in the string, the first one is replaced with the value, and the later ones are simply removed (replaced with the empty string). The sequence %% produces a single % character in the result.

Returns invalid if *format* can't be converted to a string or contains an illegal format specifier. Returns invalid if *value* can't be converted to the appropriate type.

Examples

String.format("Name: %s", "Fred")	returns string "Name: Fred"
String.format("Number: %d", 6)	returns string "Number: 6"
String.format("Speed: %f", 23.1)	returns string "Speed: 23.100000"
String.format("%7.3s", "wibble")	returns string " wib"
String.format("%7.3d", 17)	returns string " 017"
String.format("%7.3f", 5.4)	returns string " 5.400"
String.format("%s", true)	returns string "true"
String.format("%d", true)	returns string "1"
String.format("%f", true)	returns string "1.000000"
String.format("%s", "0042")	returns string "0042"
String.format("%d", "0042")	returns string "42"
String.format("%f", "0042")	returns string "42.000000"
String.format("%.f", "1.2345")	returns string "1"
String.format("%.2f%%", 1.3)	returns string "1.30%"
String.format("%%d%%f%%%d", 6)	returns string "%d%f%6"
String.format(invalid, 0)	returns invalid
String.format("%", 0)	returns invalid
String.format("%x", 0)	returns invalid
String.format("%s", invalid)	returns invalid
String.format("%d", "two")	returns invalid
String.format("%f", "six")	returns invalid

---

insertAt   Insert a new item into a list that is stored as a string

Usage

String.insertAt(*str*, *new*, *index*, *sep*)   *str* : String
new : String
index : Number
sep : String

Description

(See elementAt()'s description for an explanation of how a string is processed as a list of "elements.")

Starting with the list stored as string *str*, returns a list in which *new* has been inserted at position *index*. (The first element has index zero.) The return value is a new string; *str* itself remains unmodified.

If *index* is less than zero, *new* is added at the beginning of the list. Similarly, if *index* is past the end of the list, *new* is added at the end. Otherwise, the index of the newly inserted element is *index*. If *index* is a floating-point value, it's first converted to an integer with `Float.int()`.

Returns `invalid` if any of the arguments can't be converted to the appropriate types or if *sep* is the empty string.

Examples

```
insertAt("a;b;c;d", "x", 2, ";")        returns string "a;b;x;c;d"
insertAt("a;b;c;d", "x", -1.6, ";")     returns string "x;a;b;c;d"
insertAt("a;b;c;d", "x", 17, ";")       returns string "a;b;c;d;x"
insertAt(invalid, "x", 1, "x")          returns invalid
insertAt("foo", invalid, 2, "x")        returns invalid
insertAt("foo", "x", "three", "x")      returns invalid
insertAt("foo", "x", 4, invalid)        returns invalid
insertAt("foo", "x", 5, "")             returns invalid
```

---

isEmpty   Return true if a string is the empty string

Usage

`String.isEmpty(str)`   *str* : String

Description

Returns `true` if *str* converts to the empty string; returns `false` if it converts to a nonempty string; returns `invalid` if it can't be converted to a string.

Examples

```
String.isEmpty("")          returns boolean true
String.isEmpty("foo")       returns boolean false
String.isEmpty(123)         returns boolean false
String.isEmpty(true)        returns boolean false
String.isEmpty(2.3)         returns boolean false
String.isEmpty(invalid)     returns invalid
```

---

length   Return the length of a string

Usage

`String.length(str)`   *str* : String

Description

Returns the number of characters in string *str*; returns `invalid` if *str* can't be converted to a string.

Examples

```
String.length("foo")        returns integer 3
String.length("")           returns integer 0
String.length(42)           returns integer 2
```

```
String.length(true)                              returns integer 4
String.length(invalid)                           returns invalid
```

---

removeAt   Remove an element from a list that is stored as a string

Usage

```
String.removeAt(str, index, sep)              str : String
                                              index : Number
                                              sep : String
```

Description

(See `elementAt()`'s description for an explanation of how a string is processed as a list of "elements.")

Starting with the list stored as string `str`, returns a list with the element at position *index* removed. (The first element has index zero.) The separator is also removed, so the number of elements in the list goes down by one. The return value is a new string; *str* itself remains unmodified.

If *index* is past the end of the list, the last element is removed. Similarly, if *index* is less than zero, the first element is removed. If the string contains only one element, or is empty, an empty string is returned. If *index* is a floating-point value, it's first converted to an integer with `Float.int()`.

Returns `invalid` if any of the values can't be converted to the required types or if *sep* is the empty string.

Examples

```
String.removeAt("a;b;c;d", 2, ";")               returns string "a;b;d"
String.removeAt("a;b;c;d", -1, ";")              returns string "b;c;d"
String.removeAt("a;b;c;d", 6, ";")               returns string "a;b;c"
String.removeAt("a;b;c;d", 1.2, ";")             returns string "a;c;d"
String.removeAt("", 0, ";")                      returns string ""
String.removeAt("x", 0, ";")                     returns string ""
String.removeAt(invalid, 1, "x")                 returns invalid
String.removeAt("foo", "two", "x")               returns invalid
String.removeAt("foo", 1, invalid)               returns invalid
String.removeAt("foo", 1, "")                    returns invalid
```

---

replace   Replace all occurrences of a substring in a string with a new substring

Usage

```
String.replace(str, old, new)                 str : String
                                              old : String
                                              new : String
```

Description

Returns a string in which all occurrences of the substring *old* in the string *str* have been replaced with the substring *new*. The return value is a new string; *str* itself remains unmodified.

Returns `invalid` if any of the arguments can't be converted to a string.

Examples

```
String.replace("Hello, world!", "l", "p")   returns string "Heppo, worpd!"
String.replace("Hello, world!", "ll", "y")  returns string "Heyo, world!"
String.replace("aaaaa", "aa", "b")          returns string "bba"
String.replace(123456, 34, 43)              returns string "124356"
```

---

replaceAt

Replace an element in a list that is stored as a string

Usage

```
String.replaceAt(str, new, index, sep)
```
    str : String
    new : String
    index : Number
    sep : String

Description

(See `elementAt()`'s description for an explanation of how a string is processed as a list of "elements.")

Starting with the list stored as string *str*, returns a list in which the element at position *index* is replaced by the element *new*. (The first element has index zero.) The return value is a new string; *str* itself remains unmodified.

If *index* is less than zero, the first element is replaced. Similarly, if *index* is past the end of the list, the last element is replaced. Note that an empty *str* is a valid list with only one element: the empty string.

Returns `invalid` if any of the values can't be converted to the correct types or if *sep* is the empty string.

Examples

```
String.replaceAt("a;b;c;d", "xxx", 1, ";")    returns string "a;xxx;c;d"
String.replaceAt("a;b;c;d", "xxx", -1, ";")   returns string "xxx;b;c;d"
String.replaceAt("a;b;c;d", "xxx", 9.8, ";")  returns string "a;b;c;xxx"
String.replaceAt("", "xxx", 0, ";")           returns string "xxx"
String.replaceAt(invalid, "x", 1, "x")        returns invalid
String.replaceAt("foo", invalid, 1, "x")      returns invalid
String.replaceAt("foo", "x", "one", "x")      returns invalid
String.replaceAt("foo", "x", 1, invalid)      returns invalid
String.replaceAt("foo", "x", 1, "")           returns invalid
```

---

squeeze   Convert all whitespace within a string to a single space

Usage

```
String.squeeze(str)
```                                    *str* : String

Description

Returns a new string in which all sequences of whitespace characters in *str* have been reduced to a single space. Returns **invalid** if *str* can't be converted to a string.

Note that leading and trailing spaces aren't stripped completely; they're converted to single spaces. See the `trim()` function.

Examples

```
String.squeeze("foo")                      returns string "foo"
String.squeeze(" Once upon a time ")       returns string " Once upon a time"
String.squeeze(invalid)                    returns invalid
```

---

subString   Extract a substring from a string

Usage

```
String.subString(str, start, len)
```
str : String
start : Number
len : Number

Description

Returns a substring of *str*, starting at index *start* and continuing for *len* characters. The first character in the string has index zero.

If *start* is less than zero, it's set to zero. If there are fewer than *len* characters in the string after *start*, all are returned. If *start* is past the end of the string, or *len* is less than or equal to zero, an empty string is returned. If *start* or *len* is a floating-point number, it's first converted to an integer with `Float.int()`.

Returns **invalid** if any of the arguments can't be converted to the appropriate type.

Examples

```
String.subString("Example", 1, 2)          returns string "xa"
String.subString("Example", 4, 6)          returns string "ple"
String.subString("Example", -3, 1)         returns string "E"
String.subString("Example", 7, 2)          returns string ""
String.subString("Example", 3, -2)         returns string ""
String.subString("Example", 2.9, 3.8)      returns string "amp"
String.subString(12345, 2, 2)              returns string "34"
String.subString(false, 1, 3)              returns string "als"
String.subString(invalid, 4, 9)            returns invalid
String.subString("foo", "bar", 1)          returns invalid
String.subString("foo", 1, "bar")          returns invalid
```

---

toString

Convert any WMLScript value to a string

Usage

`String.toString(value)`   `value` : Anything

Description

Returns a string representation of `value`. If `value` is `invalid`, returns the string `"invalid"`, otherwise, returns exactly what is given by the automatic conversion of `value` to a string.

Examples

`String.toString("foo")`	returns string `"foo"`
`String.toString(17)`	returns string `"17"`
`String.toString(1.5)`	returns string `"1.5"`
`String.toString(false)`	returns string `"false"`
`String.toString(invalid)`	returns string `"invalid"`

---

trim

Remove whitespace from the beginning and end of a string

Usage

`String.trim(str)`   `str` : String

Description

Returns a new string in which any leading or trailing whitespace in `str` has been removed. Returns invalid if `str` can't be converted to a string.

Examples

`String.trim("foo")`	returns `"foo"`
`String.trim(" Once upon a time ")`	returns string `"Once upon a time"`
`String.trim(invalid)`	returns `invalid`

18

The URL Library

The URL standard library contains functions for parsing URLs, both relative and absolute. See Appendix A, *Absolute and Relative URLs*, for more on URLs and their different forms.

---

escapeString
Perform URL escaping on a string

Usage

URL.escapeString(*str*) *str* : String

Description

Returns a new string in which certain characters in *str* have been replaced with escape sequences of the form %*hh*, where *hh* is two hex digits giving the ASCII code for the value.

Returns invalid if *str* can't be converted to a string or contains characters from outside the US-ASCII character set.

Example

URL.escapeString("/foo.cgi?foo=1&bar=2") returns string
"%2Ffoo.cgi%3Ffoo%3D1%26bar%3D2"

---

getBase
Return the URL of the current WMLScript unit

Usage

URL.getBase()

Description

Returns the absolute form of the URL for the current WMLScript unit. The call part (if any) is removed, so the returned URL doesn't contain a fragment.

Example

URL.getBase()   might return string `"http://host/script.wmls"`

---

getFragment   Return the fragment extracted from a URL

Usage

URL.getFragment(*url*)   *url* : String

Description

Returns the fragment part extracted from *url*. Both absolute and relative URLs are supported. Returns the empty string if *url* doesn't include a fragment.

Returns `invalid` if *url* can't be converted to a string or can't be parsed as a URL.

Examples

URL.getFragment("#frag")   returns string `"frag"`
URL.getFragment("foo.wml#card2")   returns string `"card2"`
URL.getFragment("../logo.wbmp")   returns string `""`
URL.getFragment("http://www.inhand.net:xxx/") returns `invalid`
URL.getFragment(invalid)   returns `invalid`

---

getHost   Return the host extracted from a URL

Usage

URL.getHost(*url*)   *url* : String

Description

Returns the host part extracted from *url*. This function supports both absolute and relative URLs. Returns the empty string if *url* doesn't specify a host.

Returns `invalid` if *url* can't be converted to a string or can't be parsed as a URL.

Examples

URL.getHost("http://www.inhand.net/")   returns string `"www.inhand.net"`
URL.getHost("../logo.wbmp")   returns string `""`
URL.getHost("http://www.inhand.net:xxx/")   returns `invalid`
URL.getHost(invalid)   returns `invalid`

---

getParameters   Return the parameters extracted from a URL

Usage

URL.getParameters(*url*)   *url* : String

Description

Returns the parameters extracted from *url*. Both relative and absolute URLs are supported. Returns the empty string if *url* doesn't specify any parameters.

Returns invalid if *url* can't be converted to a string or can't be parsed as a URL.

Examples

```
URL.getParameters("http://www.inhand.net;x;y;z")    returns string "x;y;z"
URL.getParameters("http://www.inhand.net/")         returns string ""
URL.getParameters("../logo.wbmp")                   returns string ""
URL.getParameters("http://www.inhand.net:xxx/")     returns invalid
URL.getParameters(invalid)                          returns invalid
```

---

getPath   Return the path extracted from a URL

Usage

URL.getPath(*url*)   *url* : String

Description

Returns the path part extracted from *url*. This function supports both relative and absolute URLs.

Returns invalid if *url* can't be converted to a string or can't be parsed as a URL.

Examples

```
URL.getPath("http://www.inhand.net/")        returns string "/"
URL.getPath("../logo.wbmp")                  returns string "../logo.wbmp"
URL.getPath("test:")                         returns string ""
URL.getPath("http://www.inhand.net:xxx/")    returns invalid
URL.getPath(invalid)                         returns invalid
```

---

getPort   Return the port extracted from a URL

Usage

URL.getPort(*url*)   *url* : String

Description

Returns the port number extracted from *url*. Both relative and absolute URLs are supported. Returns the empty string if *url* doesn't specify a port.

Returns invalid if *url* can't be converted to a string or can't be parsed as a URL.

Examples

```
URL.getPort("http://www.inhand.net:80/")     returns string "80"
URL.getPort("http://www.inhand.net/")        returns string ""
URL.getPort("http://www.inhand.net:xxx/")    returns invalid
URL.getPort(invalid)                         returns invalid
```

getQuery   Return the query extracted from a URL

Usage

`URL.getQuery(url)`   *url* : String

Description

Returns the query part extracted from *url*. This function supports both absolute and relative URLs. Returns the empty string if *url* doesn't specify a query part.

Returns `invalid` if *url* can't be converted to a string or can't be parsed as a URL.

Examples

`URL.getQuery("http://www.inhand.net/")`	returns string `""`
`URL.getQuery("/cgi-bin/example.cgi?foo=42&bar=6")`	returns string `"foo=42&bar=6"`
`URL.getQuery("http://www.inhand.net:xxx/")`	returns `invalid`
`URL.getQuery(invalid)`	returns `invalid`

getReferer   Return the URL of whatever called this WMLScript unit

Usage

`URL.getReferer()`

Description

(Note that the spelling is "getReferer," not "getReferrer.")

Returns a relative URL to the resource that called this WMLScript unit. This URL is relative to the URL returned by `getBase()`.

The resource this URL points to may be either a WML file or another WMLScript unit. It is whatever performed the last URL call (for WML) or external function call (for WMLScript). Normal local function calls don't affect the value returned.

Example

`URL.getReferer()`   might return string `"../deck.wml"`

getScheme   Return the scheme extracted from a URL

Usage

`URL.getScheme(url)`   *url* : String

Description

Returns the scheme part of *url*. This function supports relative and absolute URLs. Returns the empty string if the URL doesn't specify a scheme.

Returns invalid if *url* can't be converted to a string or can't be parsed as a URL.

Examples

```
URL.getScheme("http://www.inhand.net/")          returns string "http"
URL.getScheme("../logo.wbmp")                     returns string ""
URL.getScheme("http://www.inhand.net:xxx/")       returns invalid
URL.getScheme(invalid)                            returns invalid
```

---

isValid   Check if a URL has valid syntax

Usage

```
URL.isValid(url)                          url : String
```

Description

Returns true if *url* has valid syntax; returns false otherwise. Valid URL syntax is summarized in Appendix A. Relative URLs are permitted.

Returns invalid if *url* can't be converted to a string.

Examples

```
URL.isValid("http://www.inhand.net/")          returns Boolean true
URL.isValid("../logo.wbmp")                     returns Boolean true
URL.isValid("#frag")                            returns Boolean true
URL.isValid("http://www.inhand.net:xxx/")       returns Boolean false
URL.isValid(invalid)                            returns invalid
```

---

loadString   Fetch a string from a URL

Usage

```
URL.loadString(url, type)                 url : String
                                          type : String
```

Description

Attempts to fetch the text resource pointed to by the URL *url*. The MIME content type of the resource must match *type*, and type must be a text type (must start with text/). If successful, the resource is converted to a string and returned. If the load fails, or the type of the resource doesn't match *type*, an integer error code is returned. This code depends on the URL scheme. For HTTP, it's an HTTP response code.

Returns invalid if either argument can't be converted to a string. Returns invalid if *type* isn't a text type or specifies more than one content type.

Examples

```
URL.loadString("http://wap.net/cgi-bin/word.cgi", "text/plain")   returns string
                                                                      "EXAMPLE"
URL.loadString("nonexistent", "text/plain")       returns integer 404
URL.loadString("foo", "text/*")                    returns invalid
URL.loadString("foo", "image/wbmp")                returns invalid
```

---

resolve   Convert a relative URL to an absolute URL

Usage

`URL.resolve(base, rel)`   *base* : String
                                                 rel : String

Description

Returns the result of resolving relative URL *rel* against the absolute base URL *base*. See Appendix A for more on URL resolving.

Returns `invalid` if either argument can't be converted to a string or can't be parsed as a URL or if the resolving fails.

Example

`URL.resolve("http://www.inhand.net/`   returns string `"http://www.inhand.net/`
    `wap/main.wml", "uk.wml")`   `wap/uk.wml"`

---

unescapeString   Undo URL escaping on a string

Usage

`URL.unescape (str)`   *str* : String

Description

Returns a new string in which all escape sequences in *str* of the form %*hh* (where *hh* is two hex digits) have been replaced with the ASCII character with hex code *hh*.

Returns `invalid` if *str* can't be converted to a string, if it contains characters from outside the US-ASCII character set, or if any of the escape sequences have hex values greater than %7F.

Example

`URL.unescapeString("%2Ffoo.cgi%3Ffoo%3D1%26bar%3D2")`   returns string `"/foo.`
                                                              `cgi?foo=1&bar=2"`

19

The WMLBrowser Library

The WMLBrowser standard library provides functions that allow WMLScript code to interact with the browser context.

At some point, there may be a way for something other than WML to invoke WMLScript functions. (This isn't the case at the time of writing, however.) If the WMLScript interpreter isn't invoked from a WML browser, each function in this library returns `invalid` and has no other effect.

---

getCurrentCard   Get the URL of the current card in the browser

Usage

```
WMLBrowser.getCurrentCard()
```

Description

Returns a relative URL pointing to the card currently displayed by the browser. This URL is relative to the URL returned by the `URL.getBase()` function.

Returns `invalid` if there's no current card in the browser.

Example

```
WMLBrowser.getCurrentCard()
```
                                                    might return `"../foo.wml#card2"`

---

getVar   Return the contents of a browser variable

Usage

```
WMLBrowser.getVar(name)
```
                                                    name : String

Description

Returns the contents of the browser variable with name *name*. If the variable isn't set, returns an empty string.

Returns `invalid` if *name* can't be converted to a string or doesn't follow the rules for variable names given in Chapter 2, *WML Variables and Contexts*.

Examples

`WMLBrowser.getVar("foo")`	returns contents of `foo`
`WMLBrowser.getVar("foo")`	returns string `""` if variable `foo` isn't set
`WMLBrowser.getVar("123")`	returns `invalid`

---

go   Specify a \<go\> task to execute

Usage

`WMLBrowser.go(url)`   *url* : String

Description

Specifies a simple \<go\> task that is executed when control returns to the browser from the WMLScript interpreter. This function, and `prev()`, may be called multiple times. Each call overrides the previous one, so only the last call to either `go()` or `prev()` has any effect. If *url* is the empty string, the resulting task has no effect. This can cancel a previous task set up with `go()` or `prev()`.

Returns the empty string; returns `invalid` if *url* can't be converted to a string.

Examples

`WMLBrowser.go("http://inhand.net/wap/main.wml")`	returns `""`
`WMLBrowser.go(invalid)`	returns `invalid`

---

newContext   Clear the browser context

Usage

`WMLBrowser.newContext()`

Description

Clears the browser context in exactly the same way as if a WML card had been entered with the `newcontext="true"` attribute.

Returns the empty string.

Example

`WMLBrowser.newContext()`

prev

Specify a <prev> task to execute

Usage

```
WMLBrowser.prev()
```

Description

Specifies a <prev> task that is executed when control returns to the browser from the WMLScript interpreter. This function, and go(), may be called multiple times. Each call overrides the previous one, so only the last call to prev() or go() has any effect.

Returns the empty string.

Example

```
WMLBrowser.prev()
```

refresh

Execute a <refresh> task

Usage

```
WMLBrowser.refresh()
```

Description

Executes a WML <refresh> task. Unlike the go() and prev() functions, the task executes immediately: it doesn't wait for control to return to the browser.

Returns the empty string.

Example

```
WMLBrowser.refresh()
```

setVar

Set a browser variable

Usage

```
WMLBrowser.setVar(name, value)
```
name : String
value : String

Description

Attempts to set the browser variable named *name* to the value given by *value*. Returns true if successful, false otherwise.

Returns invalid if either argument can't be converted to a string, or if *name* isn't a valid variable name according to the rules in Chapter 2.

Examples

```
WMLBrowser.setVar("foo", "Hello!")     sets foo to "Hello!"
WMLBrowser.setVar("123", "foo")        returns invalid
```

20

The Dialogs Library

The Dialogs standard library contains functions for putting up simple dialogs for communicating with the user.

---

alert
Display a warning message to the user

Usage

```
Dialogs.alert(msg)                          msg : String
```

Description

Displays message *msg* to the user and waits for an acknowledgement.

Returns the empty string; returns `invalid` if *msg* can't be converted to a string.

Examples

```
Dialogs.alert("Catastrophic reality failure!")
Dialogs.alert("You really didn't want to do that")
Dialogs.alert("Badness!")
```

---

confirm
Request a yes/no response from the user

Usage

```
Dialogs.confirm(msg, yes, no)               msg : String
                                            yes : String
                                            no  : String
```

Description

Displays the message *msg* and the two alternative selections *yes* and *no*, and prompts the user to select one of them. If either *yes* or *no* is the empty string, it's replaced with some implementation-dependent default value (such as `OK` or `Cancel`).

Returns `true` if the user selects the *yes* string, returns `false` if the user selects the *no* string, and returns `invalid` if any of the arguments can't be converted to a string.

Examples

```
Dialogs.confirm("Reboot Universe now?", "Yes", "No")
Dialogs.confirm("Really do it?", "OK", "Cancel")
Dialogs.confirm("Are you sure?", "", "")
```

---

prompt   Get a string from the user

Usage

```
Dialogs.prompt(msg, def)
```
                                                      msg : String
                                                      def : String

Description

Displays the message *msg* and prompts the user to enter a string. Returns whatever string the user enters or the default string *def* if the user enters no characters.

Returns `invalid` if either argument can't be converted to a string.

Example

```
Dialogs.prompt("Please enter a number", "17")
```

21

Complete Examples

The earlier chapters in this book described all the components that make up WML and WMLScript. This chapter includes several examples of how these can all be combined to create complete WAP applications with both WML and WMLScript.

One thing not covered by this chapter (or, indeed, by by this book) is the creation of dynamic WML content. This is because the techniques for doing this depend very much on the server and the language in use. Most information in any book on creating dynamic web pages is also applicable to creating dynamic WML pages, so you should simply buy a book describing whichever system you prefer, and read that in conjunction with this book. You might try *CGI Programming with Perl, Second Edition,* by Scott Guelich, Shishir Gundavaram, and Gunter Birznieks or *PHP Pocket Reference* by Rasmus Lerdorf (both published by O'Reilly & Associates).

Calculator

The first example has an interesting history. An early version of it was running in August 1998, at a time when the WAP specifications were at Version 1.0, and WMLScript had only been in the specifications for a couple of months. As a result, it's derived from what may be the first application ever to run on a WAP browser with proper integrated WMLScript. It provides a simple four-function calculator, using only WML and WMLScript.

The normal procedure for writing this sort of application is to start with the basic structure of the page in WML and add the WMLScript afterward. Example 21-1 shows the first version of the WML for this example.

Compatibility

Unfortunately, not all WAP browsers are equivalent. In particular, WMLScript support is often broken or limited. Complicated examples, such as those in this chapter, are particularly prone to incompatibilities.

The examples in this chapter have been tested on the Nokia 7110 and Ericsson R320 cell phones, on the official WAP browser for Psion PDAs, and on the WAP Developer Toolkit from Dynamical Systems Research. The examples work fine on the latter two browsers but have some problems on the two cell phones.

In particular, while both cell phones support WMLScript, there are some problems in the libraries, which means the examples don't work perfectly. The calls to the Dialogs standard library in the Battleships example are often a problem.

Some versions of the Nokia cell phone fail to handle the += and -= operators in the Calculator example. This can be fixed by replacing the line:

```
register += number;
```

with the two lines:

```
var tmp = register + number;
register = tmp;
```

even though this should have exactly the same effect according to the specifications. A similar change should be made for the -= operator.

The code in this chapter has been checked carefully against the WAP specifications and is believed to be correct.

Compatibility should improve with time, as the browsers available become more mature, and the problems of the initial rush to market become less pronounced.

Example 21-1. WML for Calculator

```
<?xml version="1.0"?>
<!DOCTYPE wml PUBLIC
    "-//WAPFORUM//DTD WML 1.1//EN"
    "http://www.wapforum.org/DTD/wml_1.1.xml">

<wml>
    <card title="Calculator" newcontext="true">
        <!-- Initialize the result variable. -->
        <onevent type="onenterforward">
            <refresh>
                <setvar name="display" value="0.0"/>
            </refresh>
        </onevent>
```

Example 21-1. WML for Calculator (continued)

```
        <!-- Result display. -->
        <p>$(display)</p>

        <!-- Rows of keys. -->
        <p>
            <a href="calc.wmls#digit(7)">7</a>
            <a href="calc.wmls#digit(8)">8</a>
            <a href="calc.wmls#digit(9)">9</a>
            <a href="calc.wmls#op('+')">+</a>
            <br/>
            <a href="calc.wmls#digit(4)">4</a>
            <a href="calc.wmls#digit(5)">5</a>
            <a href="calc.wmls#digit(6)">6</a>
            <a href="calc.wmls#op('-')">-</a>
            <br/>
            <a href="calc.wmls#digit(1)">1</a>
            <a href="calc.wmls#digit(2)">2</a>
            <a href="calc.wmls#digit(3)">3</a>
            <a href="calc.wmls#op('*')">*</a>
            <br/>
            <a href="calc.wmls#digit(0)">0</a>
            <a href="calc.wmls#point()">.</a>
            <a href="calc.wmls#op('=')">=</a>
            <a href="calc.wmls#op('/')">/</a>
        </p>
    </card>
</wml>
```

The basic structure of the page is a result display at the top, followed by four rows of four keys each. These keys are implemented using the <a> element, adding hyperlinks to characters on the page. The keys are laid out in four rows to look like the layout of keys on a simple pocket calculator.

Note also the <onvent> element, which initializes the **display** variable, so that the display looks right before any keys are pressed.

WMLScript for the Calculator

The WMLScript backend for the calculator example needs to provide the three functions referenced by the WML: **digit()** to add a digit to the number, **point()** to add a decimal point, and **op()** to perform an operation.

In addition to the **display** variable already defined, the example needs a few additional variables to emulate the behavior of a pocket calculator. Users enter a sequence of numbers with the digit and decimal point keys, separating the numbers with operators. It's conventional for the operator keys to display a running total as they go along.

The following example uses the variable **register** to store the running total: either the first number entered or the result of the last operation. It also uses both the variable **number** to store the number currently being entered, so you can keep track of whether the decimal point key has been pressed, and the variable **lastop** to store the last operator key pressed (because the operation isn't performed until after the second number is read).

Example 21-2 gives the script file for the calculator.

Example 21-2. WMLScript for Calculator

```
/*
 * WMLScript backend for calculator example.
 */


/*
 * Add a digit to the number currently being entered, and update display.
 */
extern function digit (d)
{
    /* Read the current number as a string from the browser context. */
    var number = WMLBrowser.getVar ("number");

    /* Add digit to number. (Note that the variable 'number' actually
     * contains a string at this point, so this concatenates strings.) */
    number += d;

    /* Set browser variables and refresh the display. */
    WMLBrowser.setVar ("number", number);
    set_display (Lang.parseFloat ("0" + number));
}


/*
 * Add a decimal point to the number currently being entered.
 */
extern function point ()
{
    /* Read the current number as a string from the browser context. */
    var number = WMLBrowser.getVar ("number");

    /* Ignore the key if there's already a decimal point. */
    if (String.find (number, '.') >= 0)
        return;

    /* Add a decimal point to the number. */
    number += '.';

    /* Set browser variables and refresh the display. */
    WMLBrowser.setVar ("number", number);
    set_display (Lang.parseFloat ("0" + number));
}
```

Example 21-2. WMLScript for Calculator (continued)

```
/*
 * Handle an operator key: perform the last operation and store this
 * operator until the next number has been entered.
 */
extern function op (op)
{
    /* Fetch the register and convert to floating point. */
    var register = Lang.parseFloat (WMLBrowser.getVar ("register"));

    /* Fetch the number and convert to floating point. */
    var number = Lang.parseFloat (WMLBrowser.getVar ("display"));

    /* Fetch the last operator key. */
    var lastop = WMLBrowser.getVar ("lastop");

    /* Work out what operation needs to be performed and perform it. */
    if (lastop == 'add')
        register += number;
    else if (lastop == 'sub')
        register -= number;
    else if (lastop == 'mul')
        register *= number;
    else if (lastop == 'div')
        register /= number;
    else
        register = number;

    /* Store the new operator for next time. */
    WMLBrowser.setVar ("lastop", op);

    /* Clear the number so we can enter a new one. */
    WMLBrowser.setVar ("number", "");

    /* Both the display and the register are the result of the operation. */
    WMLBrowser.setVar ("register", String.toString (register));
    set_display (register);
}

/*
 * Set the display browser variable and refresh the display.
 */
function set_display (display)
{
    /* Handle an invalid calculation result. */
    if (!isvalid display)
        display = "(error)";

    /* Set the browser variable. */
    WMLBrowser.setVar ("display", display);

    /* Refresh the display. */
    WMLBrowser.refresh ();
}
```

There are several things to note about this script file. First, the private function `set_display()` sets the `display` variable and refreshes the display, but also handles invalid values (in the case of division by zero, for example).

Second, note how each of the external functions falls into the same pattern:

1. Read variables from browser context.

2. Operate on them.

3. Write new values back into the browser context.

4. Perform a task.

In the case of this calculator, the task in Step 4 is always a refresh, and the `set_display()` function handles part of Step 3 and all of Step 4.

Finishing Off

Combining the WML of Example 21-1 and the WMLScript of Example 21-2 works, because the `newcontext` attribute on the `<card>` element clears the variables. However, it's bad practice and prone to errors to rely on this sort of behavior, so for the sake of neatness and readability, let's add three further `<setvar>` elements to the `<refresh>` task performed when the card is entered. This avoids problems if someone were to remove the `newcontext` attribute at a later date, without knowing how important it is.

Also, there is no way to correct a mistake or clear the calculation. Most pocket calculators have a **Clear** button, which resets the number currently being entered without affecting the overall calculation, and an **All Clear** button, which resets the whole calculation. These should be added to the example.

The final WML file is given in Example 21-3.

Example 21-3. Final WML for Calculator

```
<?xml version="1.0"?>
<!DOCTYPE wml PUBLIC
    "-//WAPFORUM//DTD WML 1.1//EN"
    "http://www.wapforum.org/DTD/wml_1.1.xml">

<wml>
    <card title="Calculator" newcontext="true">
        <!-- Initialize the result variable. -->
        <onevent type="onenterforward">
            <refresh>
                <setvar name="display" value="0.0"/>
                <setvar name="number" value=""/>
                <setvar name="register" value=""/>
                <setvar name="lastop" value=""/>
            </refresh>
```

Example 21-3. Final WML for Calculator (continued)

```
        </onevent>

        <!-- Result display. -->
        <p>$(display)</p>

        <!-- Rows of keys. -->
        <p>
            <a href="calc.wmls#digit(7)">7</a>
            <a href="calc.wmls#digit(8)">8</a>
            <a href="calc.wmls#digit(9)">9</a>
            <a href="calc.wmls#op('+')">+</a>
            <br/>
            <a href="calc.wmls#digit(4)">4</a>
            <a href="calc.wmls#digit(5)">5</a>
            <a href="calc.wmls#digit(6)">6</a>
            <a href="calc.wmls#op('-')">-</a>
            <br/>
            <a href="calc.wmls#digit(1)">1</a>
            <a href="calc.wmls#digit(2)">2</a>
            <a href="calc.wmls#digit(3)">3</a>
            <a href="calc.wmls#op('*')">*</a>
            <br/>
            <a href="calc.wmls#digit(0)">0</a>
            <a href="calc.wmls#point()">.</a>
            <a href="calc.wmls#op('=')">=</a>
            <a href="calc.wmls#op('/')">/</a>
            <br/>
            <anchor>C  <!-- Clear resets number being entered. -->
                <refresh>
                    <setvar name="display" value="0.0"/>
                    <setvar name="number" value=""/>
                </refresh>
            </anchor>
            <anchor>AC  <!-- All Clear resets everything. -->
                <refresh>
                    <setvar name="display" value="0.0"/>
                    <setvar name="number" value=""/>
                    <setvar name="register" value=""/>
                    <setvar name="lastop" value=""/>
                </refresh>
            </anchor>
        </p>
    </card>
</wml>
```

Exercises

To reinforce what you have learned with this example, try extending the application to add features. Easier exercises are listed first.

1. Add a memory to the calculator, with an **M** key to commit the current display to the memory, an **MC** key to clear the memory, and an **MR** key to recall the memory, replacing the current number. Do this without using any extra WML-Script.

2. Rewrite the initialization, and the handling of the **C** and **AC** keys, to use script functions instead of WML `<refresh>` tasks. When you are done there should be no tasks used in the WML except for simple `<go>` tasks.

3. Implement a percent key, so that:

    — 15 + 10% gives 16.5

    — 15 - 10% gives 13.5

    — 15 * 10% gives 1.5

    — 15 / 10% gives 150.0

    (Hint: the lines in `op()` that select which operation to perform based on the value of `lastop` also need to check `op`.)

4. Add bracket keys, and make the * and / operators have higher precedence than the + and – operators, rather than the simple left-to-right evaluation of the current example.

Battleships

The next example is a simplified version of the classic pencil-and-paper game *Battleships*. In the game, the browser puts ships randomly onto a grid, and the user selects grid cells one at a time. The browser then reports whether the guess was a hit or a miss. The aim is to sink the whole fleet in as few moves as possible.

As in the earlier example, the first thing to do is set up the WML giving the page structure. This is very regular, since all cells are handled in a similar way. Example 21-4 gives this WML. To make the example shorter, the grid has been kept to only 4×4 cells.

Example 21-4. WML for Battleships

```
<?xml version="1.0"?>
<!DOCTYPE wml PUBLIC
    "-//WAPFORUM//DTD WML 1.1//EN"
    "http://www.wapforum.org/DTD/wml_1.1.xml">

<wml>
    <card title="Battleships" newcontext="true"
        onenterforward="bships.wmls#init()">

        <!-- Display the grid. -->
        <p>
```

Example 21-4. WML for Battleships (continued)

```
            <a href="bships.wmls#guess(0,0)">$d_0_0</a>
            <a href="bships.wmls#guess(0,1)">$d_0_1</a>
            <a href="bships.wmls#guess(0,2)">$d_0_2</a>
            <a href="bships.wmls#guess(0,3)">$d_0_3</a>
            <br/>
            <a href="bships.wmls#guess(1,0)">$d_1_0</a>
            <a href="bships.wmls#guess(1,1)">$d_1_1</a>
            <a href="bships.wmls#guess(1,2)">$d_1_2</a>
            <a href="bships.wmls#guess(1,3)">$d_1_3</a>
            <br/>
            <a href="bships.wmls#guess(2,0)">$d_2_0</a>
            <a href="bships.wmls#guess(2,1)">$d_2_1</a>
            <a href="bships.wmls#guess(2,2)">$d_2_2</a>
            <a href="bships.wmls#guess(2,3)">$d_2_3</a>
            <br/>
            <a href="bships.wmls#guess(3,0)">$d_3_0</a>
            <a href="bships.wmls#guess(3,1)">$d_3_1</a>
            <a href="bships.wmls#guess(3,2)">$d_3_2</a>
            <a href="bships.wmls#guess(3,3)">$d_3_3</a>
        </p>
    </card>
</wml>
```

Note how the grid of possible guesses looks very much like the keyboard for the calculator. Each square is a hyperlink to a WMLScript function called with two arguments: the row and column of the cell.

There are differences from the calculator, however. Note how the text for each of the grid cells comes from a variable whose name contains the row and column of the cell. This regular form for the names makes the WMLScript much simpler, as you will see.

Another major difference is that the initialization isn't done with a simple `<refresh>` task. Instead, it's done via a WMLScript function called `init()`. This function is called from the `onenterforward` attribute on the `<card>` element.

WMLScript for Battleships

The WMLScript for the battleships example is quite simple. There is one initialization function, one function to handle the user guessing a square, and an additional function to congratulate the user when the game is over.

To make Example 21-5 simpler, the initialization doesn't fill the ships in randomly: the same fixed pattern is used each time.

Example 21-5. WMLScript for Battleships

```
/*
 * WMLScript for battleships game.
 */
```

Example 21-5. WMLScript for Battleships (continued)

```
/*
 * Initialize the grid. For simplicity, we don't place the ships randomly.
 * Instead, there is one fixed grid layout.
 */
extern function init ()
{
    /* Initialize all the display variables to a space. */
    for (var i=0; i<4; ++i) {
        for (var j=0; j<4; ++j) {
            WMLBrowser.setVar ("d_" + i + "_" + j, ' ');
        }
    }

    /* Initialize the secret locations of the ships. The layout looks like:
     *      * * * D
     *      D D * D
     *      * * * *
     *      B B B B
     */
    WMLBrowser.setVar ("ships", "***DDD*D****BBBB");
    WMLBrowser.setVar ("remain", 8);
    WMLBrowser.refresh ();
}


/*
 * Handle a guess at a square.
 */
extern function guess (gr, gc)
{
    /* Read the positions of the ships. */
    var ships = WMLBrowser.getVar ("ships");

    /* Read the number remaining as an integer. */
    var remain = Lang.parseInt (WMLBrowser.getVar ("remain"));

    /* Ignore this guess if user has already won. */
    if (remain == 0)
        return;

    /* Calculate the name of the cell's display variable. */
    var cellname = "d_" + gr + "_" + gc;

    /* Ignore this guess if already guessed or not on board.
     * Unguessed cells contain a space character.
     */
    if (WMLBrowser.getVar (cellname) != ' ')
        return;

    /* Find what's in the cell. */
    var hit = String.charAt (ships, 4*gr + gc);

    /* Reduce remaining ships if appropriate. */
```

Example 21-5. WMLScript for Battleships (continued)

```
    if (hit != '*')
        --remain;

    /* Update variables accordingly and refresh display. */
    WMLBrowser.setVar ("remain", remain);
    WMLBrowser.setVar (cellname, hit);
    WMLBrowser.refresh ();

    /* Congratulate the user if game is now over. */
    if (remain == 0)
        congrats ();
}


/*
 * Print congratulatory message when game won.
 */
function congrats ()
{
    /* Count number of shots required. */
    var shots = 0, hits = 0;
    for (var i=0; i<4; ++i) {
        for (var j=0; j<4; ++j) {
            var cell = WMLBrowser.getVar ("d_" + i + "_" + j);
            if (cell != ' ') {
                ++shots;
                if (cell != '*')
                    ++hits;
            }
        }
    }

    /* Calculate accuracy (proportion of shots on target). */
    var accuracy = hits / shots;

    /* Display message. */
    Dialogs.alert ("All ships sunk. "
                + String.format ("You took %d shots. ", shots)
                + String.format ("Accuracy: %.2f%%", accuracy * 100));
}
```

As the user guesses a cell, it changes from a space to either a letter (B for battleship, D for destroyer) or a star, signifying a miss. When all eight squares containing parts of ships have been hit, the `Dialogs.alert()` function informs the user. Note the use of the `String.format()` function to get precise control over the format of the floating-point percentage value.

Exercises

Once again, you should play around with this example to familiarize yourself with WML and WMLScript. The easier exercises come first.

1. Add a reset button to clear the game back to the initial state.

2. Make the grid larger.

3. Use a WML table to make the grid cells line up properly.

4. Display a running total of the number of hits and misses so far, and the percentage on target. This should update with every shot.

5. Change the initialization to put the ships in at random positions, rather than always in the same places. Put in other types of ships as well, with different sizes.

And here are some more possible enhancements. Allow the user to enter his own fleet, and have the browser shoot back at those after each of the user's shots. Put the user's fleet on one card and the current state of the browser's fleet on another, and switch between the two cards. Handle the case where the browser wins!

Absolute and Relative URLs

When URLs were originally invented, each specified everything needed to find some resource, including the protocol to use, the path to the resource, and any extra parameters required by the protocol or resource.

A URL like this is known as an *absolute URL*, because it contains all this information. It can be passed around freely without needing any extra context to fetch its resource.

Absolute URLs are a problem, however, when you have a group of resources that all reference each other, such as the group of web pages that make up a complete web site. If you want to move this site to a different server, you have to go through every page looking for URLs on the old server, and change these to point to the new server.

The problem can occur even without moving the pages from one server to another. Many people test their web sites locally on their own computer, using *file URLs*. If these sites use absolute URLs for their cross references, all the links have to be changed before the site can be uploaded to the main server. (Apart from being inconvenient, this is also a place where errors can be introduced.)

The solution to this problem is to allow parts of the URL to be omitted. Such partial URLs are known as *relative URLs*. Alone, they don't contain enough information to locate a resource; they must be converted into absolute URLs by adding the missing parts. This process is known as *resolving*.

A URL is resolved relative to an existing absolute URL, which determines the correct values for the missing parts. This *base URL*, as it's known, is usually the URL of the resource containing the relative URL. For example, the URL of an image within a WML card is resolved relative to the URL of the card containing the reference.

Parts of a URL

To understand how resolving works, it is first necessary to learn the terms used for the different parts of a URL and how they are extracted from the URL. These parts are, in the order they appear in the URL:

scheme:
> The type of the URL. This is necessary to know how to interpret the other components. All absolute URLs must have a scheme.

//network
> Gives the network information for network-based protocols. This contains the address of the server, and any login and password information required to connect. For example, for HTTP URLs, this is the hostname or Internet address of the server.

/path
> Gives the path of the resource. The leading / may be omitted if no network information is given. (The / is actually treated as part of the path, so strictly speaking *file://foo* and *file:foo* are not the same. The first is a file *foo* in the root directory, while the second is a file *foo* in the current directory. However, many implementations treat both forms as relative to the root directory.)

;parameters
> Gives optional extra parameters that may be used by some URL schemes. The parameters are a list of values separated by *;* characters. For example, an FTP URL can take a parameter *type=d* to indicate that the URL represents a directory and not just a file. Parameters are rarely used.

?query
> An optional part of the URL that represents some sort of query to be sent to the referenced resource. For example, web pages using server-side processing often send arguments after a ? character.

#fragment
> Used in certain cases to reference part of a resource. For example, the cards within a WML deck are referenced using the fragment part.

At minimum, a URL needs a scheme. Most schemes also require the URL to have a path, and network-based schemes usually require a network location. Some URL schemes don't follow these rules exactly, but those that don't can't be used with relative URLs.

Examples

As an example of how these parts work together, take the URL:

> *file://homes/martin/foo.wml*

This is a simple URL with a scheme of *file* and a path of */homes/martin/foo.wml*. No other parts are present.

For a more complicated example, consider:

> *http://www.wap.net/cgi-bin/wapmail.cgi?m=1#msg3*

In this example, the scheme is *http*, the network information is *www.wap.net,* the path is */cgi-bin/wapmail.cgi*, the query is *m=1*, and the fragment is *msg3*.

Resolving Relative URLs

The process of resolving a relative URL into an absolute URL has many rules, but only a few are often useful:

- If the relative URL has a scheme, it's interpreted as a complete absolute URL by itself. This means you can always put an absolute URL anywhere you put a relative one.

  For example, given the base URL *http://www.wapforum.org/*, the URL *http://wap.net/main.wml* (which is actually an absolute URL) resolves to *http://wap.net/main.wml*.

- If the relative URL consists of nothing but a fragment, the new URL is simply the entire base URL with the fragment from the relative URL.

  For example, given the base URL *file:/homes/martin/foo.wml,* the relative URL *#card2* resolves to *file:/homes/martin/foo.wml#card2*.

- If the relative URL has no scheme or network information, the scheme and network information from the base URL are used, together with the parameters, query, and fragment from the relative URL. In addition, the path from the relative URL is interpreted in a special way:

  — If it starts with a / character, it's used as it is: the full path from the relative URL is appended to the scheme and network parts from the base URL.

  — Otherwise, the paths from the base and relative URLs are each treated as a list of parts separated by / characters. The last part of the base URL's path is removed and replaced with the path from the relative URL.

    Any parts consisting entirely of the character . are removed. Parts consisting of the characters .. are also removed, along with the part before them. This allows a relative URL to effectively change the directory of the URL. (You can think of . as meaning the current directory, and .. meaning the parent directory.)

If you use Unix, you may recognize this as similar to the way that paths to files are interpreted. A / character at the beginning of a pathname indicates the root directory, which in this case means the web server's top-level directory; a pathname that doesn't begin with a / is interpreted relative to the directory of the current page. MS-DOS and Microsoft Windows behave in a similar way but use the \ character instead of /.

Examples

For example, given the base URL:

> *http://wap.net/examples/hangman/main.wml*

various relative URLs resolve as follows:

page.wml
> *http://wap.net/examples/hangman/page.wml*

/page.wml
> *http://wap.net/page.wml*

img/img0.wbmp
> *http://wap.net/examples/hangman/img/img0.wbmp*

./img/img0.wbmp
> *http://wap.net/examples/hangman/img/img0.wbmp*

.///////img/img0.wbmp
> *http://wap.net/examples/hangman/img/img0.wbmp*

../calc/main.wml
> *http://wap.net/examples/calc/main.wml*

/cgi-bin/word.cgi
> *http://wap.net/cgi-bin/word.cgi*

B

WAP Gateways and WSP

When visiting a site on the Web, a user's browser connects directly to the web server to load the page. The browser must perform certain tasks, such as converting server names into numeric server addresses. The server must output the content in exactly the form required by the browser.

WAP puts additional demands on the server side. WML and WMLScript files aren't transmitted in their original text format but in a compacted, encoded format. This means that some text-to-binary processing is required before data is sent to the browser. WAP also uses a different protocol for the actual data transfer. The standard HTTP protocol used on the Web is quite inefficient in terms of the number of bytes that transmit the message headers. WAP uses a terser protocol, called the *Wireless Session Protocol* (WSP).

Fortunately, it's not necessary to modify existing web servers to support these differences. Data from a standard web server is passed through a software filter, called a *WAP gateway*, which handles both the protocol change and the text-to-binary conversion. This means that any of the normal server-side technologies used on the Web can create WAP content, too—CGI scripts, Java servlets, PHP scripts, and so on.

WSP Headers

If you've done any advanced development for the Web, you probably know about *HTTP headers*. These are pieces of information passed to the browser along with the response content. Since WSP is designed to replace HTTP, you may expect that WSP also provides headers, and you'd be right. These headers can be specified on a response using the <meta> element in WML (see Chapter 6, *WML Decks*,

Templates, and Cards)—specifically the `http-equiv` form. The WMLScript `meta` pragma can also specify headers (see Chapter 14, *WMLScript Pragmas*).

There are many headers: most are used only for low-level communication and aren't useful for you to set directly. These include headers giving the length of the contents, for example. This information is calculated for you by the WAP gateway, so there's no need to do it yourself.

Headers related to *caching* are useful, however. As you may know, web browsers keep a local cache of responses, to save on repeated network activity fetching the same page or image again and again. WAP browsers also do this, and the caching headers allow you to control how an item is cached, how long it can be kept, and even whether it's cached at all.

Browser Support for Caching

Unfortunately, support for caching headers (or indeed many headers at all) is very poor in WAP browsers at the time of this writing. This means that pages may be cached even when you specifically request them not to be. To get around this, many sites insert a random number into the URL and set up the server to ignore this. Because the number changes from request to request, the browser treats each repeated request as if it were a new request.

For example, suppose there's some information that changes regularly at the URL:

/news/headlines.wml

You can add a header that prevents the page from being cached at all, using the `http-equiv` form of the `<meta>` element in WML:

```
<meta http-equiv="Cache-Control" value="no-cache"/>
```

However, the browser may well ignore these header. To get around this, make the browser add a randomly chosen number to the URL requesting the page:

/news/headlines.wml?9832077283

Set up your web server to ignore this number and just serve the same page, and your caching problems go away. (The Apache web server does this by default.)

C

Summary of WMLScript Operators

Operator	Operation	Operands	Result
Precedence: 1 (highest) / Associativity: none			
++	Increment	Number	Number or invalid
--	Decrement	Number	Number or invalid
+	Unary plus	Number	Number or invalid
−	Unary minus	Number	Number or invalid
~	Bitwise not	Integer	Integer or invalid
!	Logical not	Boolean	Boolean or invalid
typeof	Get datatype	Any	Integer
isvalid	Check if valid/invalid	Any	Boolean
Precedence: 2 / Associativity: left			
*	Multiplication	Number, number	Number or invalid
/	Floating-point division	Float, float	Float or invalid
div	Integer division	Integer, integer	Integer or invalid
%	Remainder	Integer, integer	Integer or invalid
Precedence: 3 / Associativity: left			
+	Addition or string concatenation	Number/string, number/string	Number or string or invalid
−	Subtraction	Number, number	Number or invalid

Operator	Operation	Operands	Result
Precedence: 4 / Associativity: left			
<<	Shift left	Integer, integer	Integer or invalid
>>	Shift right (signed)	Integer, integer	Integer or invalid
>>>	Shift right (unsigned)	Integer, integer	Integer or invalid
Precedence: 5 / Associativity: left			
<	Less than	Number/string, number/string	Boolean or invalid
<=	Less than or equal to	Number/string, number/string	Boolean or invalid
>	Greater than	Number/string, number/string	Boolean or invalid
>=	Greater than or equal to	Number/string, number/string	Boolean or invalid
Precedence: 6 / Associativity: left			
==	Equal to	Number/string, number/string	Boolean or invalid
!=	Not equal to	Number/string, number/string	Boolean or invalid
Precedence: 7 / Associativity: left			
&	Bitwise and	Integer, integer	Integer or invalid
Precedence: 8 / Associativity: left			
^	Bitwise exclusive or	Integer, integer	Integer or invalid
Precedence: 9 / Associativity: left			
|	Bitwise or	Integer, integer	Integer or invalid
Precedence: 10 / Associativity: left			
&&	Logical and	Boolean, boolean	Boolean or invalid
Precedence: 11 / Associativity: left			
||	Logical or	Boolean, boolean	Boolean or invalid
Precedence: 12 / Associativity: left			
?:	Conditional	Boolean, any, any	Any

Operator	Operation	Operands	Result
Precedence: 13 / Associativity: right			
=	Assignment	Variable, any	Any
*=	Assignment with multiplication	Variable, number	Number or invalid
/=	Assignment with floating-point division	Variable, float	Float or invalid
div=	Assignment with integer division	Variable, integer	Integer or invalid
%=	Assignment with remainder	Variable, integer	Integer or invalid
+=	Assignment with addition or concatenation	Variable, number/string	Number or string or invalid
-=	Assignment with subtraction	Variable, number	Number or invalid
<<=	Assignment with left shift	Variable, integer	Integer or invalid
>>=	Assignment with right shift (signed)	Variable, integer	Integer or invalid
>>>=	Assignment with right shift (unsigned)	Variable, integer	Integer or invalid
&=	Assignment with bitwise and	Variable, integer	Integer or invalid
|=	Assignment with bitwise or	Variable, integer	Integer or invalid
Precedence: 14 / Associativity: left			
,	Sequential evaluation	Any, any	Any

D

Serving WAP Content from a Standard Web Server

All the popular web servers can be configured easily to serve WAP content. In most cases, all that is required is to add a few extra content-type mappings to the server.

Most web servers work out the content type of the data in their responses from the extension (suffix) on the filename. For example, a server may have a mapping that all files ending in *.jpg* or *.jpeg* have content type `image/jpeg`, and all files ending with *.htm* or *.html* have content type `text/html`.

To serve WML and WMLScript from a standard web server, therefore, it's necessary to teach the server some new filename extensions and content types. The types that need to be added and the common extensions for them appear in Table D-1.

Table D-1. WAP Content Types

File Type	MIME Type	Extension
WML source	`text/vnd.wap.wml`	*.wml*
WMLScript source	`text/vnd.wap.wmlscript`	*.wmls*
WBMP image	`image/vnd.wap.wbmp`	*.wbmp*
WML binary	`application/vnd.wap.wmlc`	*.wmlc*
WMLScript binary	`application/vnd.wap.wmlscriptc`	*.wmlsc*

The last two rows in the table, the binary forms of WML and WMLScript, aren't as important as the others. They are useful only if you have access to a WML encoder or WMLScript compiler and want to preconvert your content. (This is a fairly advanced thing to do.) It won't do any harm to have them in the server even if you don't use them, though.

The method for actually adding these mappings to the server depends on the server software. Most commercial web servers have some sort of graphical or web-based configuration interface that does this sort of thing. Consult the user's manual or your local expert.

If you're using the free web server Apache, simply add the following five lines to the end of the *mime.types* file in the configuration directory, and then restart the server:

```
text/vnd.wap.wml                wml
text/vnd.wap.wmlscript          wmls
image/vnd.wap.wbmp              wbmp
application/vnd.wap.wmlc        wmlc
application/vnd.wap.wmlscriptc  wmlsc
```

Index

About the Author

Martin Frost is the head of WAP technology at Digital Mobility Ltd. in London, United Kingdom. He has been working with WAP since 1998 and has written a complete WAP browser and worked on the design of a WAP gateway. He has a degree in math and computing from Imperial College, London. He spends his free time reading, playing cricket, designing ever more elaborate schemes to wire up his home and his car, planning world domination, and trying to find time to actually do all these things....

Colophon

Our look is the result of reader comments, our own experimentation, and feedback from distribution channels. Distinctive covers complement our distinctive approach to technical topics, breathing personality and life into potentially dry subjects.

The insect on the cover of *Learning WML and WMLScript* is a mosquito (*nematocera culicidae*).

The mosquito is a flying, bloodsucking insect best known, and even feared, for its biting and spreading of disease. There are approximately 2,500 species of mosquitoes in the world, with over 150 species in North America.

Mosquitoes usually live close to a water source because the larva must develop in water, which can be anything from a running stream to stagnant water in a birdbath. Depending on the species, a mosquito's life span is between two weeks and a few months. Some can hibernate at temperatures below 50 degrees F, but others can't survive in temperatures that low.

Only female mosquitoes bite; males do not. Females must bite because they need blood to develop their eggs. They bite once per batch of eggs, and a female can lay several batches in her lifetime, which multiplies into many generations of mosquitoes per year. Both sexes feed primarily on nectar and other plant and fruit liquids.

Mosquitoes are attracted to humans, and other mammals, by the carbon dioxide exhaled when breathing. Other factors also contribute, such as body odor, body heat, and sweat, and sometimes perfumes, deodorants, and detergents.

Mosquito bites are more than just itchy and annoying, however. The real potential danger is that mosquitoes can be carriers and transmitters of many serious diseases such as malaria, yellow fever, encephalitis, and the West Nile virus in humans, heartworm in dogs, and Eastern equine encephalitis in horses. As a result, there are many efforts all over the world to control mosquito populations.

Mary Anne Weeks Mayo was the production editor and copyeditor for *Learning WML and WMLScript*. Nicole Arigo proofread the book. Rachel Wheeler, Emily Quill, and Jane Ellin provided quality control. John Bickelhaupt wrote the index.

Ellie Volckhausen designed the cover of this book, based on a series design by Edie Freedman. The cover image is an original illustration created by Lorrie LeJeune. Emma Colby produced the cover layout with QuarkXPress 4.1 using Adobe's ITC Garamond font.

Alicia Cech and David Futato designed the interior layout based on a series design by Nancy Priest. Mike Sierra implemented the design in FrameMaker 5.5.6. The text and heading fonts are ITC Garamond Light and Garamond Book; the code font is Constant Willison. The illustrations that appear in the book were produced by Robert Romano using Macromedia FreeHand 8 and Adobe Photoshop 5. This colophon was written by Nicole Arigo.

Whenever possible, our books use a durable and flexible lay-flat binding. If the page count exceeds this binding's limit, perfect binding is used.

O'REILLY®

O'Reilly & Associates, Inc.
101 Morris Street
Sebastopol, CA 95472-9902
1-800-998-9938

Visit us online at:
www.oreilly.com
order@oreilly.com

O'REILLY WOULD LIKE TO HEAR FROM YOU

Which book did this card come from?

_____

Where did you buy this book?
- ❏ Bookstore
- ❏ Direct from O'Reilly
- ❏ Bundled with hardware/software
- ❏ Other _____

- ❏ Computer Store
- ❏ Class/seminar

What operating system do you use?
- ❏ UNIX
- ❏ Windows NT
- ❏ Other _____

- ❏ Macintosh
- ❏ PC(Windows/DOS)

What is your job description?
- ❏ System Administrator
- ❏ Network Administrator
- ❏ Web Developer
- ❏ Other _____

- ❏ Programmer
- ❏ Educator/Teacher

❏ Please send me O'Reilly's catalog, containing a complete listing of O'Reilly books and software.

Name _____ Company/Organization _____

Address _____

City _____ State _____ Zip/Postal Code _____ Country _____

Telephone _____ Internet or other email address (specify network) _____

Nineteenth century wood engraving
of a bear from the O'Reilly &
Associates Nutshell Handbook®
Using & Managing UUCP.

BUSINESS REPLY MAIL
FIRST CLASS MAIL   PERMIT NO. 80   SEBASTOPOL, CA

Postage will be paid by addressee

O'Reilly & Associates, Inc.
101 Morris Street
Sebastopol, CA 95472-9902